Classroom Integration of Type II Uses of Technology in Education

Classroom Integration of Type II Uses of Technology in Education has been co-published simultaneously as *Computers in the Schools*, Volume 22, Numbers 3/4 2005.

Monographic Separates from *Computers in the Schools*

For additional information on these and other Haworth Press titles, including descriptions, tables of contents, reviews, and prices, use the QuickSearch catalog at http://www.HaworthPress.com.

Classroom Integration of Type II Uses of Technology in Education, edited by Cleborne D. Maddux, PhD, and D. LaMont Johnson, PhD (Vol. 22, No. 3/4, 2005). *"Anyone interested in fulfilling the potential of instructional technology will benefit from this work. . . . Explores Type II technologies from the perspectives of a series of astute observers." (David Richard Moore, PhD, Assistant Professor, Educational Studies/Instructional Technology, Ohio University, Athens)*

Internet Applications of Type II Uses of Technology in Education, edited by Cleborne D. Maddux, PhD, and D. LaMont Johnson, PhD (Vol. 22, No. 1/2, 2005). *An overview of effective Type II teaching applications that use technology to develop new and better strategies for learning.*

Web-Based Learning in K-12 Classrooms: Opportunities and Challenges, edited by Jay Blanchard, PhD, and James Marshall, PhD (Vol. 21, No. 3/4, 2004). *Examines the possibilities of today's online learning applications across the K-12 curriculum.*

Integrating Information Technology into the Teacher Education Curriculum: Process and Products of Change, edited by Nancy Wentworth, PhD, Rodney Earle, PhD, and Michael L. Connell, PhD (Vol. 21, No. 1/2, 2004). *A powerful reference for teacher education departments striving to integrate new technologies into their curriculum and motivate their faculty to utilize them.*

Distance Education: What Works Well, edited by Michael Corry, PhD, and Chih-Hsuing Tu, PhD (Vol. 20, No. 3, 2003). *"A must read. . . . Provides a highly readable, practical, yet critical perspective into the design, delivery, and implementation of distance learning. . . . Examines issues faced by distance educators, offers valuable tactics culled from experience, and outlines strategies that have been key success factors for a wide variety of distance learning initiatives." (Veena Mahesh, PhD, Distance and Blended Learning Program Manager, Technology Manufacturing Group Training, Intel Corporation)*

Technology in Education: A Twenty-Year Retrospective, edited by D. LaMont Johnson, PhD, and Cleborne D. Maddux, PhD (Vol. 20, No. 1/2, 2003). *"Interesting, informative, relevant. . . . Having so many experts between the covers of one book was a treat. . . . I enjoyed reading this book!" (Susan W. Brown, PhD, Science/Math Methods Professor and Professional Curriculum Coordinator, New Mexico State University)*

Distance Education: Issues and Concerns, edited by Cleborne D. Maddux, PhD, Jacque Ewing-Taylor, MS, and D. LaMont Johnson, PhD (Vol. 19, No. 3/4, 2002). *Provides practical, research-based advice on distance education course design.*

Evaluation and Assessment in Educational Information Technology, edited by Leping Liu, PhD, D. LaMont Johnson, PhD, Cleborne D. Maddux, PhD, and Norma J. Henderson, MS (Vol. 18, No. 2/3 and 4, 2001). *Explores current trends, issues, strategies, and methods of evaluation and assessment in educational information technology.*

The Web in Higher Education: Assessing the Impact and Fulfilling the Potential, edited by Cleborne D. Maddux, PhD, and D. LaMont Johnson, PhD (Vol. 17, No. 3/4 and Vol. 18, No. 1, 2001). *"I enthusiastically recommend this book to anyone new to Web-based program development. I am certain that my project has moved along more rapidly because of what I learned from this text. The chapter on designing online education courses helped to organize my programmatic thinking. Another chapter did an outstanding job of debunking the myths regarding Web learning." (Carol Swift, PhD, Associate Professor and Chair of the Department of Human Development and Child Studies, Oakland University, Rochester, Michigan)*

Using Information Technology in Mathematics Education, edited by D. James Tooke, PhD, and Norma Henderson, MS (Vol. 17, No. 1/2, 2001). *"Provides thought-provoking material on several aspects and levels of mathematics education. The ideas presented will provide food for thought for the reader, suggest new methods for the classroom, and give new ideas for further research." (Charles E. Lamb, EdD, Professor, Mathematics Education, Department of Teaching, Learning, and Culture, College of Education, Texas A&M University, College Station)*

Integration of Technology into the Classroom: Case Studies, edited by D. LaMont Johnson, PhD, Cleborne D. Maddux, PhD, and Leping Liu, PhD (Vol. 16, No. 2/3/4, 2000). *Use these fascinating case studies to understand why bringing information technology into your classroom can make you a more effective teacher, and how to go about it!*

Information Technology in Educational Research and Statistics, edited by Leping Liu, PhD, D. LaMont Johnson, PhD, and Cleborne D. Maddux, PhD (Vol. 15, No. 3/4, and Vol. 16, No. 1, 1999). *This important book focuses on creating new ideas for using educational technologies such as the Internet, the World Wide Web and various software packages to further research and statistics. You will explore on-going debates relating to the theory of research, research methodology, and successful practices.* Information Technology in Educational Research and Statistics *also covers the debate on what statistical procedures are appropriate for what kinds of research designs.*

Educational Computing in the Schools: Technology, Communication, and Literacy, edited by Jay Blanchard, PhD (Vol. 15, No. 1, 1999). *Examines critical issues of technology, teaching, and learning in three areas: access, communication, and literacy. You will discover new ideas and practices for gaining access to and using technology in education from preschool through higher education.*

Logo: A Retrospective, edited by Cleborne D. Maddux, PhD, and D. LaMont Johnson, PhD (Vol. 14, No. 1/2, 1997). *"This book–honest and optimistic–is a must for those interested in any aspect of Logo: its history, the effects of its use, or its general role in education." (Dorothy M. Fitch, Logo consultant, writer, and editor, Derry, New Hampshire)*

Using Technology in the Classroom, edited by D. LaMont Johnson, PhD, Cleborne D. Maddux, PhD, and Leping Liu, MS (Vol. 13, No. 1/2, 1997). *"A guide to teaching with technology that emphasizes the advantages of transiting from teacher-directed learning to learner-centered learning–a shift that can draw in even 'at-risk' kids." (Book News, Inc.)*

Multimedia and Megachange: New Roles for Educational Computing, edited by W. Michael Reed, PhD, John K. Burton, PhD, and Min Liu, EdD (Vol. 10, No. 1/2/3/4, 1995). *"Describes and analyzes issues and trends that might set research and development agenda for educators in the near future." (Sci Tech Book News)*

Language Minority Students and Computers, edited by Christian J. Faltis, PhD, and Robert A. DeVillar, PhD (Vol. 7, No. 1/2, 1990). *"Professionals in the field of language minority education, including ESL and bilingual education, will cheer this collection of articles written by highly respected, research-writers, along with computer technologists, and classroom practitioners." (Journal of Computing in Teacher Education)*

Logo: Methods and Curriculum for Teachers, by Cleborne D. Maddux, PhD, and D. LaMont Johnson, PhD (Supp #3, 1989). *"An excellent introduction to this programming language for children." (Rena B. Lewis, Professor, College of Education, San Diego State University)*

Assessing the Impact of Computer-Based Instruction: A Review of Recent Research, by M. D. Roblyer, PhD, W. H. Castine, PhD, and F. J. King, PhD (Vol. 5, No. 3/4, 1988). *"A comprehensive and up-to-date review of the effects of computer applications on student achievement and attitudes." (Measurements & Control)*

Educational Computing and Problem Solving, edited by W. Michael Reed, PhD, and John K. Burton, PhD (Vol. 4, No. 3/4, 1988). *Here is everything that educators will need to know to use computers to improve higher level skills such as problem solving and critical thinking.*

The Computer in Reading and Language Arts, edited by Jay S. Blanchard, PhD, and George E. Mason, PhD (Vol. 4, No. 1, 1987). *"All of the [chapters] in this collection are useful, guiding the teacher unfamiliar with classroom computer use through a large number of available software options and classroom strategies." (Educational Technology)*

Computers in the Special Education Classroom, edited by D. LaMont Johnson, PhD, Cleborne D. Maddux, PhD, and Ann Candler, PhD (Vol. 3, No. 3/4, 1987). *"A good introduction to the use of computers in special education. . . . Excellent for those who need to become familiar with computer usage with special population students because they are contemplating it or because they have actually just begun to do it." (Science Books and Films)*

You Can Do It/Together, by Kathleen A. Smith, PhD, Cleborne D. Maddux, PhD, and D. LaMont Johnson, PhD (Supp #2, 1986). *A self-instructional textbook with an emphasis on the partnership system of learning that introduces the reader to four critical areas of computer technology.*

Computers and Teacher Training: A Practical Guide, by Dennis M. Adams, PhD (Supp #1, 1986). *"A very fine . . . introduction to computer applications in education." (International Reading Association)*

Classroom Integration of Type II Uses of Technology in Education

Cleborne D. Maddux
D. LaMont Johnson
Editors

Classroom Integration of Type II Uses of Technology in Education has been co-published simultaneously as *Computers in the Schools*, Volume 22, Numbers 3/4 2005.

Routledge
Taylor & Francis Group
NEW YORK AND LONDON

First Published by

The Haworth Press, Inc., 10 Alice Street, Binghamton, NY 13904-1580.

Transferred to digital printing in 2011 by Routledge
711 Third Avenue, New York, NY 10017
2 Park Square, Milton Park, Abingdon, Oxon, OX14 4RN

Classroom Integration of Type II Uses of Technology in Education has been co-published simultaneously as *Computers in the Schools*, Volume 22, Numbers 3/4 2005.

Cover design by Katie Johnson

Library of Congress Cataloging-in-Publication Data

Classroom integration of Type II uses of technology in education / Cleborne D. Maddux, D. LaMont Johnson, editors.
p. cm.
"Co-published simultaneously as Computers in the schools, volume 22, numbers 3/4, 2005."
Includes bibliographical references and index.
ISBN-13: 978-0-7890-3110-5 (hard cover : alk. paper)
ISBN-10: 0-7890-3110-8 (hard cover : alk. paper)
ISBN-13: 978-0-7890-3111-2 (soft cover : alk. paper)
ISBN-10: 0-7890-3111-6 (soft cover : alk. paper)
1. Educational technology–United States. 2. Information technology–United States. 3. Computer-assisted instruction–United States. I. Maddux, Cleborne D., 1942- II. Johnson, D. LaMont (Dee LaMont), 1939- III. Computers in the schools.
LB1028.3.C618 2005
371.33–dc22

2005013548

Classroom Integration of Type II Uses of Technology in Education

Contents

T . TF	nn /	1	TAT	TT C	
IN	IR(	) ( ) (	UC^{-}	11(	

Information Technology, Type II Classroom I and the Limited Infrastructure in Schools	ntegration,	
	orne D. Maddux LaMont Johnson	1
An Examination of Gender Differences in Ele Constructionist Classrooms Using Lego/Lo	•	
	Sally R. Beisser	7
Early Algebra with Graphics Software as a Ty of Technology	pe II Application	
Se	rgei Abramovich	21
Defining and Applying Idea Technologies: A Conceptual Framework for Teachers	Systematic,	
Mar	yanne R. Bednar John J. Sweeder	35
The Technology Integration Assessment Instru Understanding Planned Use of Technology by Classroom Teachers		
	Jody S. Britten	
J_{i}	errel C. Cassadv	49

ABOUT THE EDITORS

Cleborne D. Maddux, PhD, is Foundation Professor in the Department of Counseling and Educational Psychology at the University of Nevada, Reno, where he teaches courses on statistics and on integrating technology into education. He has co-authored 10 books with D. LaMont Johnson, including *Distance Education: Issues and Concerns* and the textbook *Educational Computing: Learning with Tomorrow's Technologies*, now in its third edition.

D. LaMont Johnson, PhD, Professor of Educational Technology in the College of Education at the University of Nevada, Reno (UNR), is a leading specialist in the area of educational computing and related technologies. He is the founding editor of *Computers in the Schools* and is Program Coordinator of the Information Technology in Education program at UNR. He has co-authored 10 books, including *Distance Education: Issues and Concerns* and the textbook *Educational Computing: Learning with Tomorrow's Technologies*, now in its third edition. A popular speaker and conference presenter, Dr. Johnson is active in several professional organizations concerned with advancing the use and understanding of educational technology.

INTRODUCTION

Cleborne D. Maddux
D. LaMont Johnson

Information Technology, Type II Classroom Integration, and the Limited Infrastructure in Schools

SUMMARY. In this second special issue on Type II applications of information technology in education, the focus is on classroom integration. This editorial explores some possible explanations for the fact that information technology in schools has not fulfilled its considerable potential. One reason may be that individualized instruction is not part of the subculture of public schooling. This, in turn, may have been caused by the lack of a widespread and effective instructional infrastructure in schools. However, some educators have been able to implement Type II

CLEBORNE D. MADDUX is Associate Editor for Research, *Computers in the Schools,* and Foundation Professor, Department of Counseling and Educational Psychology, University of Nevada, Reno, Reno, NV 89557 (E-mail: maddux@unr.edu).
D. LAMONT JOHNSON is Professor, Department of Counseling and Educational Psychology, College of Education, University of Nevada, Reno, Reno, NV 89557 (E-mail: ljohnson@unr.edu).

[Haworth co-indexing entry note]: "Information Technology, Type II Classroom Integration, and the Limited Infrastructure in Schools." Maddux, Cleborne D., and D. LaMont Johnson. Co-published simultaneously in *Computers in the Schools* (The Haworth Press, Inc.) Vol. 22, No. 3/4, 2005, pp. 1-5; and: *Classroom Integration of Type II Uses of Technology in Education* (ed: Cleborne D. Maddux, and D. LaMont Johnson) The Haworth Press, Inc., 2005, pp. 1-5. Single or multiple copies of this article are available for a fee from The Haworth Document Delivery Service [1-800-HAWORTH, 9:00 a.m. - 5:00 p.m. (EST). E-mail address: docdelivery@haworthpress.com].

Available online at http://www.haworthpress.com/web/CITS

doi:10.1300/J025v22n03_01

applications of information technology in their educational settings, even without such an infrastructure. The present special issue presents articles by such individuals.

KEYWORDS. Type II, information technology in education, classroom integration, infrastructure, individualized instruction

This is the second part of a three-part series of special double issues of *Computers in the Schools*. The entire series is dedicated to articles dealing with *Type II* applications of information technology in education. This particular issue will include articles that focus on *classroom integration* of Type II applications. (The first issue dealt with Type II applications that are Internet-related.)

As we explained in the lead article of the first special issue, the concept of Type I and Type II applications of information technology in education goes back to the early 1980s, when we were young professors at Texas Tech University in Lubbock, Texas. As the result of a completely unlikely and accidental, yet opportune, series of coincidences, we found ourselves surrounded by a number of energetic and talented colleagues with an intense interest in exploring the potential of small computers to improve teaching and learning.

One of those colleagues was Jerry Willis, who was at the time finishing a book entitled *Computers for Everybody*–a volume that proved so visionary and influential that it became the only book placed on permanent display in the computer section of the *Smithsonian*. Jerry went on to found *SITE*, the *Society for Information Technology and Teacher Education*, and to author more books than the entire faculty of most university departments. He is currently distinguishing himself as he pursues a new passion–studying and helping to develop the use of information technology in education as it occurs in other countries.

There were at least half a dozen other technology enthusiasts on that faculty, although Jerry was clearly the de facto leader. Unfortunately, as so often happens, the college leadership at the time was unable or unwilling to recognize a unique opportunity, and one by one, nearly all these individuals moved on to other positions.

It was before that happened, however, that we began to discuss and to write about how we should begin to bring computers into schools. As we talked with colleagues about the potential of information technology, we began to think in terms of a dichotomy of educational applications. We began to call them *Type I* or *Type II* applications. *Type I* applications are those uses that simply make it faster, easier, or otherwise more convenient to continue teaching or learning in traditional ways, while *Type II* applications are those uses that make it possible to teach or learn in new and better ways. While Type I uses are beneficial to teachers and learners, it is Type II applications that we believe hold the greatest potential for contributing meaningfully to education.

As previously mentioned, Type II applications are the focus of the present series of three special issues of *Computers in the Schools*, and the specific focus of this particular issue are those Type II applications that represent *classroom integration*. Although educators have been talking about classroom integration of information technology since the beginning of the modern computer movement, true integration remains an elusive goal. Virtually every modern authority who has written on the topic has concluded that, while there are some noteworthy exceptions, computers are generally poorly used in schools, are not integrated meaningfully into classroom activities, and are far from achieving their potential.

It is ironic that since the early 1980s, the quality of the technology itself has improved in gigantic leaps forward in sophistication, power, and affordability, while curriculum integration in today's typical classrooms has progressed only marginally, if at all. There is no shortage of opinions about why this is so. Thousands of articles and hundreds of volumes have been written attempting to explain the lag between the quality of technology and the quality of classroom technology applications.

There is probably no one answer to the question of why the gap is so large. There are undoubtedly many contributing factors. However, in considering this question, we are continually drawn to considering the lack of progress toward *individualized instruction*. Educators have been advocating individualization for much longer than we have been educators. However, we seem no closer today to realizing this goal than we have ever been.

Thus, the problem, it seems to us, is much more a problem in the subculture of teaching and learning, than one of technological sophistication or even public policy. The potential of computers, it seems to us, is due to their unique ability to incorporate interaction, and thus to individualize instruction. If the subculture of teaching and learning is not consistent with individualization, then true classroom integration cannot take place. This, we believe, is the situation today.

This brings up the questions of why individualization of teaching and learning has been a popular topic, but a difficult goal. Again, there are undoubtedly many reasons, but we believe that one of them is that schools have a severely limited infrastructure to support instruction. In fact, it might be said that there is *no* supporting infrastructure whatsoever in the typical public school. Nearly every employee provides direct services all day to children, thereby leaving little or no time for instructional support activities such as authoring or selecting curriculum materials or planning and carrying out research or program evaluations. Only a few employees do not face children for hours on a daily basis. The principal is one of these, but he or she is typically so busy responding to bureaucratic demands and to an ever-increasing legion of single-issue, special interest groups that there is usually no time or inclination to engage in professional support activities. The secretary generally acts as personal assistant to the principal, and maintenance staff members are responsible only for the physical facilities.

Contrast this situation with infrastructure with that found in medicine, for example. For every primary care physician, there is a host of specialists, technicians, paraprofessionals, and aides, and the drug companies and the Federal Government make sure that needed research and development activities take place.

While education probably needs considerably less supporting infrastructure than does medicine, we suspect that education cannot move meaningfully toward widespread individualization with the current, near-nonexistent supportive infrastructure. Additionally, events at the national level, such as recent federal education legislation will likely make the chances of building an effective educational infrastructure even less likely in the near future than it has been in the past. After all, *No Child Left Behind* is essentially an assessment and accountability law that contains built-in punitive measures, and no funding for educational infrastructure.

What will be the future of computing in schools in the absence of individualization in the subcultures of teaching and learning? Computers have so much cultural momentum that they will continue to appear in schools, but they are unlikely to become part of the actual fabric of teaching and learning, and they are equally unlikely to revolutionize either activity. In short, they may not become instruments of Type II teaching and learning. They will likely remain in the Type I category, merely making it faster, easier, or more convenient in other ways to continue teaching and learning in traditional ways.

That is the bad news. The good news is that there *are* exceptions to this dismal picture of lost potential. There are classrooms in which individualization of teaching and learning, in the words of George Kneller (1965), is part of the *manifest*, rather than merely the *ideal* culture.

The articles in this special issue are by individuals who have managed to employ information technology in schools in ways to make possible new and better strategies of teaching and learning–strategies that would not be available without that technology. That they have been able to do so in the absence of an extensive and effective educational instructional infrastructure proves that such an accomplishment is possible. We offer these articles in the hope that others will be persuaded to find ways to integrate Type II applications of information technology into their own classrooms.

REFERENCE

Kneller, G. F. (1965). *Educational anthropology: An introduction.* New York: Wiley & Sons.

Sally R. Beisser

An Examination of Gender Differences in Elementary Constructionist Classrooms Using Lego/Logo Instruction

SUMMARY. Gender disparity exists in many educational environments despite conscientious attempts to equalize opportunities and outcomes. Research studies indicate females are less likely to effectively engage in the use of technology for problem solving. However, in a two-year study of a Midwest elementary multi-age classroom, researchers studied computer-using activity of grade 1-5 students using Lego/Logo technologies. Teachers put in practice learning strategies that encouraged both sexes to engage in computer-oriented problem solving. Through an experimental design, observation, and teacher assessment, the results suggest that, in practice, females demonstrate significant gains in self-efficacy using computer technology in this computer-rich classroom and report positive perceptions of self. Girls report more positive assessments of female technological competence and current computer use while boys do not waver from a belief in male technological superiority. Observation and teacher assessment indicate females are solving problems without asking for help. Furthermore, girls suggest that males are not more technologically savvy than they are.

SALLY R. BEISSER is Associate Professor, Teaching and Learning Department, School of Education, Drake University, Des Moines, IA 50311 (E-mail: sally.beisser@drake.edu).

[Haworth co-indexing entry note]: "An Examination of Gender Differences in Elementary Constructionist Classrooms Using Lego/Logo Instruction." Beisser, Sally R. Co-published simultaneously in *Computers in the Schools* (The Haworth Press, Inc.) Vol. 22, No. 3/4, 2005, pp. 7-19; and: *Classroom Integration of Type II Uses of Technology in Education* (ed: Cleborne D. Maddux, and D. LaMont Johnson) The Haworth Press, Inc., 2005, pp. 7-19. Single or multiple copies of this article are available for a fee from The Haworth Document Delivery Service [1-800-HAWORTH, 9:00 a.m. - 5:00 p.m. (EST). E-mail address: docdelivery@haworthpress.com].

Available online at http://www.haworthpress.com/web/CITS

doi:10.1300/J025v22n03_02

Girls also indicate that boys were not more likely to be adult computer users. On the other hand, boys report only a slight shift in their gendered beliefs.

KEYWORDS. Lego/Logo technologies, effective strategies of computer-using teachers, computers and female competence

STATEMENT OF THE PROBLEM

Gender disparity exists in educational environments despite conscientious attempts to equalize opportunities and outcomes. Sex differences persist in attainment of careers in the related fields of mathematics, science, and technology (AAUW, 1998; Beisser, 1999-2000; Meece & Eccles, 1993; Roblyer, 2000; Sutton, 1991; Turkle, 1988; Wellesley College Center for Research on Women, 1992). Much effort has been expended to change the patterns of attitudes and behaviors that lead to unequal outcomes (AAUW, 1998; Fennema, 1990; Kahle & Meece, 1994).

Despite gains in policy inviting equal opportunity for females such as Title IX initiatives (1997), academic status and opportunities lag for girls in use of technology. The American Association of University Women report, *Gender Gaps: Where Schools Still Fail Our Children* (1998), indicates that females still lag behind males in their interest in computer studies, enrollment in computer courses, and decisions to major in computer sciences. Women remain underrepresented in technology-based careers, such as engineering, computer studies, and medicine (Klein & Ortman, 1994; Mark, 1992). If females are to be full participants in their learning environments and in the workplace, they must possess basic and necessary technology skills and knowledge for participation and advancement.

RECOMMENDATIONS FROM THE LITERATURE

Recommendations from a study of adolescent females (Beisser, 1999, p. 4) strongly recommend cultivating early childhood experiences and school exposure to computers for activities requiring logic, reasoning, and higher level thinking in order to encourage girls to use technology. Use of technology is compromised in classrooms that do not foster problem solving. Casey and Tucker (1994) found successful classrooms are focused on problem-based and planning strategies more systematically and intensely than is the case in most classrooms. Creative students are constantly questioning and curious, enjoy figuring things out, seek out challenges, are persistent, approach tasks in a flexible way, are self-reliant, and feel confident about themselves as learners and risk takers. Students who are effective planners think things through before they act, gather, and organize materials in an appropriate way, and systematically approach different parts of the task.

The teacher's role in a problem-centered classroom is critical. "Children are natural question-askers. But whether they continue to ask questions–and especially to ask good questions–depends largely on how adults respond to their questions" (Sternberg, 1994, *Phi Delta Kappan*, p. 136). Not every teacher teaches problem solving. Moursand (2002) asserts the notion that "every teacher teaches problem solving" is a haphazard approach to learning, and that the result is that most students do *not* get a coherent introduction to problem solving. Learners must have a clearly defined initial situation, a clearly defined goal (a desired end situation), a clearly defined set of resources, and ownership to use knowledge, skills, and energies to achieve the desired final goal. In response to these findings, and with clear understanding of effective pedagogy, five teachers in one multi-age school have found something that works.

EFFECTIVE USE OF COMPUTERS IN A "CONSTRUCTIONIST" CLASSROOM

Constructivism is loosely defined in educational literature, referring to ill-defined concepts such as constructing knowledge, creating meaningful learning, problem solving, reflective construction, or metacognition (Maddux & Cummings, 1999). Despite vague understanding and implementation of constructivist theory, many teachers have been drawn to better practices whether they clearly understood the term or not. However, the teachers in this study moved from *constructivist* generalizations to *constructionist* (Harel & Papert, 1991) theory and practice. Constructionism is a theory of learning based on two different notions of *construction* of knowledge. First, it is grounded on the idea that children learn by actively constructing new knowledge, not by having information dispensed to them (Piaget, 1924). Second, constructionism asserts that effective learning takes place when the learner is engaged in constructing personally meaningful artifacts using manipulatives such as creating computer animations, robots, plays, poems, icons, objects, or pictures representing one's own learning. As a collaborator in this research initiative, Seymour Papert, Massachusetts Institute of Technology (MIT) professor, has dedicated his retirement years to help teachers and students use Lego®/Logo technologies as intelligent manipulative tools to nourish children's active construction of knowledge. This study results from Dr. Papert's influence and leadership with interim visits with the teachers and children in this research project.

Learning with computers and using the Logo programming language is a daily activity for approximately 100 students in one, grade 1-5 elementary school. Children in each of these five classrooms have daily blocks of time to work in a technology-rich environment filled with Mindstorms™ kits and MicroWorlds® for constructing and programming, thinking and problem solving, developing and sharing expertise. Papert developed the Logo computer language in the 1970s as an "intelligent tool" to develop logical thinking and reasoning. The Lego® Company marketed Mindstorms™ kits, so named after Papert's seminal book (1980). Using Legos® as intelligent tools, children build machines out of the Lego® pieces, connect their machines to a computer, and write Logo programs to control the machines. With MicroWorlds® software, students use mathematics for creating pictures, animations, music, games, and simulations on the computer. Papert says, "Given a good programming language, I see children struggling to make a program work in a way that they seldom sweat at their paper-and-pencil mathematics" (1999, p. 4). Papert promotes computers as "*Children's Machines*" in his work on *Rethinking School in the Age of the Computer* (1993).

RESEARCH QUESTIONS

Four research questions driving this study were: (a) Do elementary girls and boys demonstrate different learning behaviors as they respond to multiple computer programming activities in a computer-rich classroom? (b) Does a computer-rich environment enhance female competence or confidence in using computer technologies? (c) Do boys view themselves as more competent or confident than girls in using computer technologies? (d) Do teachers use instructional or management strategies that enhance self-efficacy of students in a computer-rich environment?

METHODOLOGY

Participants

All students ($N = 99$) in the grade 1-5 school completed a two-page questionnaire designed to assess student attitudes about using technology for learning and relevance of technology in learning and future work. Classroom teachers and university research assistants helped students understand directions, responded to any questions, and occasionally assisted in spelling words in the written response section. Students in grades one and two worked in small groups to respond to the survey questions while the upper grades completed the survey as a whole class. Five classroom teachers were observed for ways in which they designed and assessed classroom activities using computer technologies, promoted problem solving using Lego/Logo programming, and interacted with their elementary students.

Instruments

The student questionnaire (obtainable from the senior author at address sally.beisser@drake.edu) consisted of 20 questions with responses based on a four-point Likert-like scale. Response categories were 1 = strongly disagree, 2 = disagree, 3 = agree, and 4 = strongly agree. In addition, three narrative responses described a "positive experience with computers," a "frustrating experience with computers," and designation of "someone who was good at using computers." Questionnaires were developed in conjunction with the teachers and were administered by the teachers during the fall and spring semester of the 2001-2002 school year. Survey data were analyzed in SPSS. Use of t-tests allowed analysis of specific attitudinal changes in girls and boys as well as comparisons by gender. A second instrument, a teacher observation form allowed researchers to conduct weekly observations of teacher-to-student interaction and instruction using computer technology in effective ways. The observation form served as a cross check sheet to determine instructional techniques that represent the most frequently observed behaviors from all participating teachers.

Procedures

Data from interviews with the five teachers were analyzed qualitatively to extract instructional strategies typifying behaviors that resulted in positive learning experiences in the classroom. Furthermore, the research team observed and categorized the teaching and management strategies of the teachers using 30-minute observational periods to cross check teacher reports. Researchers, including graduate and undergraduate students, collected data in weekly visits to the grade 1-5 multi-age classroom for a two-year observational study. By examining sex-based learning activities in a classroom using computers for problem solving, researchers investigated possible differences in student behavior using the construction and programming materials in a technology-rich school.

METHODS OF DATA ANALYSIS

Qualitative Results

Indeed, elementary girls and boys demonstrate different learning behaviors in a computer-rich classroom as addressed in research question (a). Even with the same construction and building materials and programming instruction and high expectations for all students, females responded differently from the males. Females were initially intent on building stereotypical structures such as houses and social settings. Girls were content to make aesthetically pleasing structures such as houses with rooms. They needed specific encouragement from the teachers to use the materials to build and program structures to function using moving parts. In time, however, they were successful in programming structures to move. Males, on the other hand, made things move from the onset, even if structures were loosely constructed and were easily demolished upon impact. Females more readily worked in pairs or teams, while males worked more independently or alone in daily activities. Females were more inclined to refer to written directions in the Lego/Logo booklets that accompanied the building components. Males were more likely to assemble pieces as they invented final products that moved with wheels and gears. In completing required "progress folios" to describe student accomplishments of the day, females were more meticulous in writing down or drawing their action steps, detailing what they had learned in relation to programming, than males who used fewer words in the analysis of their progress. However, both males and females valued extra time to complete their projects and responded with a collective groan when it was time to put the construction and computer programming materials away. It seems clear that females responded favorably to increased attention to skill-building competence and the development of personal confidence as a result of the technology-rich classroom environment as addressed in research question (b).

In addition, elementary students responded to effective teaching strategies (research question d) that invite all children, especially the females, to become more efficacious problem solvers. From interviews with the teachers and observations of their direct work with the students, 11 strategies have emerged that, while aimed at all students, specifically assisted the females in using computer technology in effective ways. The following teacher behaviors were evident through the weekly observations of the teachers in the technology-rich school with a high investment in tenacious learning episodes of the students. Of these 11 teacher strategies, 8 were general instructional strategies, while 3 were specific to enhancing gender competencies.

General teaching strategies using technology effectively. Extended Time. Teachers use relatively long lengths of time for students to sustain work on existing technology projects. When students were deep in thought and planning, teachers allowed them to continue work on projects after the perceived time of closure. Teachers planned in advance for longer periods of time for extended technology projects to be developed. *Inviting Complex Tasks.* Teachers direct students to make multiple-page MicroWorlds projects with animation or increased complexity in design. They require kids to "go beyond" or take the next steps to "make something move" in Lego/Logo or MicroWorlds, thus inviting programming opportunities. *Purposeful Grouping of Students.* Teachers group "females with females," linking those with more experience and pair students with expertise with younger students for support in using Lego/Logo and MicroWorlds programs. They also group "females with males" with programming and Lego/Logo experience, and expertise as pairs. *Longer Processing or Wait Time.* Teachers employ longer wait time after asking questions to get a response from students. They also wait longer after getting a response before moving on to more conversation or questioning. They give kids obvious time to process ideas or to think about their learning. *Students Acting as Experts.* Teachers engage students in assisting others as the "expert" when using technology. Teachers promote student expertise, rather than the teacher as expert. *Probing Questions.* Teachers thoughtfully ask probing questions such as, Can you tell me about what you are doing? Explain what you just did. How does this work? Was this successful? Why or why not? What will you try next? Show me how this goes? Was there a problem that you solved? If so did that solve a problem? What will you try next? Why do you think this will work? *Authentic Assessment*. Journaling and reflection are daily experiences. Teachers manage "Progress Folios" that include reflective journaling and representation of work and problem-solving experiences that are kept over time. Goals are established at peer-led parent/teacher conferences in the fall and spring and are agreed upon by the student, parent, and teacher. *Positive Technology Self-Talk from Teachers*. Teachers convey their own success levels/positive experiences with features of Lego/Logo and MicroWorlds programs technology (e.g., troubleshooting success). Teachers portray a general positive attitude using technology (not related to the Lego/Logo and MicroWorlds) such as remaining positive in the face of crashes, memory loss, programming problems, or technical problems, or when troubleshooting does not work.

Gender specific strategies in using technology effectively. Encouraging Construction Behavior for Both Genders. Teachers encourage both boys and girls, as individuals, to build with Lego/Logo or other construction materials in clearly defined situations that promote a desired end situation using a clearly defined set of resources, and ownership to use knowledge, skills, and energies to achieve the desired final goal. *Specific Female Encouragement*. Teachers direct female students to construct or program (e.g., make a vehicle, construct something that is "stronger" or that won't crash when you operate it). For example, they ask girls to program a construction with the "yellow brick." Generally, they encourage girls to move away from stereotypical constructs such as a "house, flowers, etc.," or at least to implement programming with these designs. *Whole Group Talks on Gender Diversity and/or Individual Differences*. Teachers organize group conversations about gender-related issues, such as talking about individual differences that exist in the world, or hold class meetings about gender issues specifically. These may be teacher directed or student initiated. They give all students a chance to express opinions with regard to differences in the large group setting.

According to the study's qualitative accounts, girls are thriving in this environment. One teacher said, "When we first started Lego/Logo computer work in our class, the girls played with the Lego building blocks to make only houses and families. But now, we are observing that girls not only work with gears and motors and pulleys just like the boys do, but express intentions to use programming language." Females in this study are experiencing success using computer technology for learning and creative activity, and express intentions for future use of technology. Outcomes from the study include documentation of student success and self-efficacy of females in the classroom using computer technology in meaningful ways.

Males are thriving too. However, the primary difference is that they continue to think they are very competent in using technology for problem solving at school as well as in their futures. They consider themselves to be superior to the girls, but the girls do not see it this way. They report that their competence is strong and they do not report needing to be helped in the face of technological challenges and view themselves as equally competent computer-users at school as well as in the future. Boys continue to create vehicles that crash, and upon demolition, recreate them and reprogram them. They are still consulted as experts more frequently than the females, but girls disagree that the boys hold the market on expertise. Even if the girls create stereotypical scenes such as "Happy Joes" pizza kitchens, a bakery, amusement rides in a theme park, they are making moveable operations through programming.

Quantitative Results

Research question (c) compared both male and female competence and confidence in using computer technologies in their classrooms. There were observable differences. Table 1 indicates significant pretest differences between girls and boys on seven of the ten technological learning relevance items. It was evident that neither group believed that computer use was gendered, but girls were less supportive (girls' mean = 1.76; boys' mean = 2.41). However, when it came to adult computer use, boys and girls believed that they would be more likely than their counterparts to use computers. Boys reported more agreement that they used computers to build things more so than girls did (boys' mean = 3.08; girls' mean = 2.56). On average, boys reported that males played with computer games more than girls did (mean = 2.83), but girls disagreed (mean = 2.16). The groups disagreed on boys being more technologically sophisticated than girls were (boys' mean = 2.61; girls' mean = 1.85). Boys believed that girls asked for technological help more (mean = 2.80), while girls did not think so (mean = 1.81).

In general, boys held attitudes that were favorable to their own sex, with the exception of computer use in childhood. For the most part, girls did not buy into boys' technological superiority. However, when it

TABLE 1. Relevance of Technology for Learning and Future Work (Pretest Findings)

	Boys		Girls		Mean Difference	*t*	*p*
	M	*SD*	*M*	*SD*			
1. Boys use computers more often than girls do.	2.41	1.22	1.76	1.03	0.65	2.800	0.006
2. Boys play with more computer games than girls do.	2.83	1.17	2.16	1.15	0.67	2.806	0.006
3. Boys use computers more than girls to build moving things or use motors.	3.08	1.17	2.56	1.10	0.52	2.213	0.029
4. Girls ask for help more often than boys in using technology.	2.80	1.16	1.81	1.02	0.99	4.246	0.000
5. Boys are better at using technology than girls.	2.61	1.20	1.85	1.01	0.76	3.386	0.001
6. Boys are more likely than girls to use computers when they grow up.	2.90	1.19	2.00	1.19	0.90	3.676	0.000
7. Girls are more likely than boys to use computers when they grow up.	1.85	.97	2.67	1.33	−0.82	−3.315	0.002

came to girls being more likely to have a partner or less likely to use mechanical skills with computers, gendered expectations persisted. These gender differences persisted throughout the study. When comparing mean pretest and posttest differences in girls' and boys' attitudes, there was only one statistically significant change. In the final analysis, both sexes reported that girls were *not* more likely to use computers in their adult lives. It may be the case that girls developed more realistic attitudes about their own future technological use while boys shifted to less negative views toward females' competency (girls' mean change = −.33; boys' mean change = .24).

For girls, there were positive attitudinal shifts about female competency. At the close of the spring semester, girls no longer believed that boys used mechanical skills with computers more than they did (pretest mean = 2.61; posttest = 2.03). They were firmly convinced that boys were not more technologically sophisticated (pretest mean = 1.83;

posttest mean = 1.36). They were resolute in their position that boys were not more likely to use computers as adults (pretest mean = 2.00; posttest mean = 1.58). In regard to boys' attitudes about the relevance of technology, their views did not shift from time 1 to time 2.

Comparisons of pretest and posttest results revealed that boys and girls did not differ in the way they felt about using computer technologies at home or at school. No statistically significant changes were noted in boys' attitudes over time. Girls only differed on one variable. They evidenced less support for using MicroWorlds every day at school (pretest mean = 3.26; posttest mean = 2.71) at completion of the study.

IMPLICATIONS FOR FEMALES

Our study suggests that both sexes are thriving in this Lego/Logo environment. Both groups view computer use as important for completing schoolwork and for future job or career roles. In contrast to studies in the literature of males holding dominance as computer users, females in this classroom report that they "think they can" be competent in using technology. However, boys remained convinced of their own technological superiority. Boys held to their beliefs that *they* played more with games and motors, didn't ask for help very much, and were generally better at using computers than girls, and were more likely to use computers in the future. Boys reported a slight reduction in their negative views of females. On the other hand, this intervention helped girls eliminate some of their gendered beliefs. Girls reported that they were just as capable with technology and the construction of motorized computer projects as boys, and as adults, that boys would not dominate computer use. Girls gained new confidence in their use of technology and more realistic expectations. It seems promising that the grade 1-5 girls in this study will refuse to be "marginalized" in later grades, such as middle school and high school, or even in future life experiences using the computer. However, continued interventions are critical to the development of skills, competencies, attitudes, and decision-making of females for success in later years.

Finally, these findings may benefit teachers in contemporary classrooms as they make meaningful and lasting impressions on elementary learners, particularly females, as they use technology for problem solving. The teacher's role in a problem-centered classroom is absolutely critical. Moursand (2002) asserts that teachers tend not to teach problem solving, as is frequently assumed. However, intentional use of computer technology with clearly defined goals to think through problems, gather and organize materials, and systematically approach tasks has the potential to empower students to learn differently according to this study. Effective teacher strategies influence children's ability to ask questions, take risks, figure things out, plan ahead, seek challenges, become persistent, develop self-reliance, and approach their work in a flexible manner. In addition, these strategies invite females to use their intellectual abilities. Importantly this approach allows males to acknowledge that girls can program, design structures, and analyze operations. In summary, because effective use of technology is central to the mission of many educational institutions, this study suggests that females are competent using computers for problem-solving programming activities at a young age and that teachers are important to the development of individual potential to use computers effectively in a classroom environment.

REFERENCES

AAUW. (1998). *Gender gaps: Where schools still fail our children.* Washington, DC: American Association of University Women Educational Foundation.

Beisser, S. R. (1999). *Constructivist environments inviting computer technology for problem-solving: New junctures for female students.* Unpublished doctoral dissertation, Iowa State University, Ames, IA.

Beisser, S. R. (1999-2000, Winter). Females and technology: Lack of equity for gifted adolescent females. *National Association for Gifted Children Computers and Technology Division, NAGC Newsletter*, Washington, DC.

Casey, M. B., & Tucker, E. C. (1994). Problem-centered classrooms: Creating lifelong learners. *Phi Delta Kappan, 76*(2), 139-143.

Fennema, E. (1990). Justice, equity and mathematics education. In F. Fennema & G. Leder (Eds.), *Mathematics and gender* (pp. 1-9). New York: Teachers College Press.

Harel, I., & Papert, S. (1991). *Constructionism.* Norwood, NJ: Ablex.

Klein, S., & Ortman, P. (1994, November). Continuing the journey toward gender equity. *Educational Researcher, 23*(8), 13-21.

Kahle, J. B., & Meece, J. L . (1994). Research on gender issues in the classroom. In D. Gabel (Ed.), *Handbook of research in science teaching and learning* (pp. 542-557). Washington, DC: National Science Teachers Association.

Maddux, C. D., & Cummings, R. (1999). Constructivism: Has the term outlived its usefulness? *Computers in the Schools, 15*(3/4), 5-10.

Mark, J. (1992, June). Beyond equal access: Gender equity in learning with computers. *Women's Educational Equity Act Publishing Center Digest*, 5-9.

Meece, J. L., & Eccles, J. S. (1993). Introduction: Recent trends in research on gender and education. *Educational Psychologist, 28*(4), 313-319.

MicroWorlds 2.03®. (1997). Highgate Springs, VT: Logo Computer Systems Inc. Retrieved September 8, 2004, from http://www.lcsi.ca.
MicroWorlds Pro®. (2000). Highgate Springs, VT: Logo Computer Systems Inc. Retrieved September 8, 2004, from http://www.lcsi.ca.
Lego® MindStorms™. (1998). Enfield, CT: LEGO Systems, Inc. Retrieved September 8, 2004, from http://legomindstorms.com.
MIT Epistemology and Learning Group. (2000). Retrieved September 8, 2004, from http://el.www.media.mit.edu/groups/el/elProjects.html.
Moursand, D. G. (2002, October 28). *Brief introduction to roles of computers in problem-solving.* Retrieved November 8, 2002, from University of Oregon, Oregon Technology in Education Council: http://darkwing.uoregon.edu/~moursund/SPSB/
Papert, S. (1980). *Mindstorms: Children, computers and powerful ideas.* New York: Basic Books.
Papert, S. (1993). *The children's machine: Rethinking school in the age of the computer.* New York: Basic Books.
Papert, S. (1999). *Vision-making, new technologies, and powerful ideas in education.* A talk at Heartland Area 11 Educational Agency/Drake University, Des Moines, IA: April 30, 1999.
Piaget, J. (1924). *Judgment and reasoning in the child.* Atlantic Heights, NJ: Humanities Press.
Roblyer, M.D. (May, 2000). Digital desperation: Reports on a growing technology and equity crisis. *Learning and Leading with Technology, 27*(8), 50-61.
Sternberg, R. J. (1994). Answering questions: Questioning answers. *Phi Delta Kappan, 76*(2), 136-138.
Sutton, R. E. (1991). Equity and computers in the schools: A decade of research. *Review of Educational Research, 61*, 475-503.
Title IX at 25: Report card on gender equity. (1997, June). National Coalition for Women and Girls in Education.
Turkle, S. (1988). Computational reticence: Why women fear the intimate machine. In C. Kramarae (Ed.), *Technology and Women's Voices.* New York: Routledge & Kegan Paul.
Wellesley College Center for Research on Women. (1992). *The AAUW report: How schools shortchange girls.* Washington, DC: American Association of University Women.

Sergei Abramovich

Early Algebra with Graphics Software as a Type II Application of Technology

SUMMARY. This paper describes the use of Kid Pix–graphics software for creative activities of young children–in the context of early algebra as determined by the mathematics core curriculum of New York state. It shows how grade-two appropriate pedagogy makes it possible to bring about a qualitative change in the learning process of those commonly struggling with mathematics by substituting computer-mediated tasks for algebraic tasks. The pedagogy is analyzed along the lines of Vygotsky's theory of using tools and signs in the internalization of higher psychological functions.

KEYWORDS. Graphics software, informal reasoning, early algebra, problem solving, zone of proximal development, mediated cognition

SERGEI ABRAMOVICH is Professor, School of Education and Professional Studies, State University of New York at Potsdam, Potsdam, NY 13676-2294 (E-mail: abramovs@potsdam.edu).

Gratitude is expressed to Beverly Smith (formerly of SUNY Potsdam) for cooperation during the field-testing of activities described in this paper. Special thanks are extended to Debra Brice, curriculum coordinator, Randy Sanders, technology coordinator, and the second-grade students who participated in this project–all of Hermon-DeKalb Elementary School, DeKalb Junction, NY.

[Haworth co-indexing entry note]: "Early Algebra with Graphics Software as a Type II Application of Technology." Abramovich, Sergei. Co-published simultaneously in *Computers in the Schools* (The Haworth Press, Inc.) Vol. 22, No. 3/4, 2005, pp. 21-33; and: *Classroom Integration of Type II Uses of Technology in Education* (ed: Cleborne D. Maddux, and D. LaMont Johnson) The Haworth Press, Inc., 2005, pp. 21-33. Single or multiple copies of this article are available for a fee from The Haworth Document Delivery Service [1-800-HAWORTH, 9:00 a.m. - 5:00 p.m. (EST). E-mail address: docdelivery@haworthpress.com].

Available online at http://www.haworthpress.com/web/CITS

doi:10.1300/J025v22n03_03

The teacher must orient his work not on yesterday's development in the child but on tomorrow's.

–L. S. Vygotsky

One of the major themes of today's mathematics education research is the impact of computer technology on K-12 classrooms. This impact was recognized more than a decade ago in an ambitious agenda for teaching mathematics in North American schools presented in the National Council of Teachers of Mathematics' *Curriculum and Evaluation Standards for School Mathematics* (National Council of Teachers of Mathematics, 1989). The *Standards* called for students "to use the computer as a tool for processing information and performing calculations to investigate and solve problems" (p. 8). The position of the 1989 document was advanced in its more recent version *Principles and Standards for School Mathematics* (National Council of Teachers of Mathematics, 2000)–by elevating technology to the status of being a principle: "Technology is essential in teaching and learning mathematics; it influences the mathematics that is taught and enhances students' learning" (p. 24). These statements clearly point to the fact that technology brings about significant changes in K-12 mathematics education by raising students' intellectual abilities to higher ground.

One may note that, in a more general context, Maddux (1994) had made a distinction between ways technology can be used in educational applications and advocated for "new and better methods of teaching and learning . . . that would not be available without technology" (p. 31). Maddux argued that bringing technology into education is so expensive in terms of time, effort, and enthusiasm, that the expenditure can only be justified if it brings about a qualitative change in how we teach and learn. Hence the term *Type II applications of technology* was coined. The main feature of Type II applications is that of giving students control of almost everything that happens on the screen, including student-computer interaction. It is through such an interaction that tools of technology can serve as "intellectual partners . . . in order to engage and facilitate critical thinking and higher-order learning" (Jonassen, 1996, p. 9). Through Type II applications of technology, students' cognitive processes and their development can become more visible to the teacher so that the potential for providing help in a social milieu of the classroom can be realized. By the same token, students can assist one another, when appropriate, working in a collaborative learning environment of a computerized classroom (Means, 1994).

This paper describes the use of graphics software with second-graders of a rural school in upstate New York in a highly sophisticated (for that grade level) problem-solving context. Maddux, Johnson, and Willis (1997) defined graphics software as a program that enables one to draw pictures on the computer screen. These authors argued that graphics software can be considered as Type II if its instructional uses stimulate one's active intellectual involvement into technology-enabled tasks and provide opportunities for spontaneous and open-ended interaction with the software. Regardless of grade level, solving nonroutine problems in mathematics is a clear-cut example of such an intellectual activity. Therefore, using graphics software in support of nonroutine mathematical problem solving is a Type II application of technology. This paper shows how one can adapt versatile features of Kid Pix (Broderbund Software, Inc., 2001) for fostering young children's informal mathematical reasoning skills in the context of what may be construed as an early application-oriented algebra. The context was artificially developed through recognizing that various seemingly unrelated, applied problem-solving tasks across the K-12 mathematics core curriculum of New York state are structurally identical and thus can be embedded into a single, grade-two appropriate context. The use of the software by young children is analyzed through Vygotsky's (1978) construct of using tools and signs in the internalization of higher psychological functions.

RECURRING MATHEMATICAL STRUCTURE IN NEW YORK STATE CORE CURRICULUM

Dienes (1960), one of the early advocates for continuity in teaching mathematics, argued that any mathematical structure once introduced is used later in other parts of the curriculum. More recently, Connell (2001) suggested that mathematical thinking of young children in developmentally appropriate (e.g., action-oriented) environments may parallel higher level lines of thought of developmentally more advanced learners. These pedagogical positions are reflected, though implicitly, in a resource guide (New York State Education Department, 1998) that provides guidance to districts and schools in New York state for structuring local mathematics curricula and instruction. Problems 1 through 3 that follow are applied algebra problems found in the guide. Pertaining to the elementary, middle, and secondary levels, respectively, the problems illustrate how the same mathematical structure hidden in diverse contextual situations reoccurs in different parts of the curriculum across grades. Appropriate use of technology can bridge pedagogy of different grade levels. It should be noted that, while teachers are encouraged to use technology in all parts of the curricula, no specific recommendations are provided in the guide in connection with the problems. As will be shown below, the use of graphics software could play a major role in mathematical development of young children, preparing them for participating in more advanced activities as they grow older.

Problem 1 (recommended for grade 2). *A pet store sold only birds and cats. One day the store's owner asked his clerk to count how many animals there were in the store. The clerk counted 18 legs. How many cats and birds might there have been?*

Problem 2 (recommended for middle school). *Julie sold 125 frozen juice bars and 150 ice cream cones on Saturday. She made a total of $500. Julie sold each ice cream cone for $2.25. Write an equation you can use to find the cost of each frozen juice bar. Solve the equation you wrote to find the cost of one frozen juice bar.*

Problem 3 (recommended for high school). *Mary purchased 12 pens and 14 notebooks for $20. Carlos bought 7 pens and 4 notebooks for $7.50. Find the price of one pen and the price of one notebook algebraically.*

Analyzing the three problems, one can recognize that, regardless of context, a similar structure is recurring across grades. It is based on linear combinations of contextually related objects put in two groups according to their specific properties. More specifically, such objects are cats and birds, frozen juice bars and ice cream cones, and finally, pens and notebooks. Three main didactical differences among the three problems can be recognized: the context, the magnitude of the numbers involved, and a number system used at each grade level. This implies that all three problems can be introduced at the primary level provided that the context, magnitude, and number system are grade appropriate. To this end, the following two problems were designed as the conversion of the middle and secondary school problems, respectively, into primary school problems. Artificial names *trimp* and *grimp* given to the creatures are vicarious variables (or informal unknowns–the number of legs that each creature has) to be used at an early elementary level.

Problem 2.1. *Julie, a pet store's owner, sold two types of animals on Saturday; two of them were cats and three of them were some other type of animal. She counted 23 legs. How many legs did the other animal have?*

Problem 3.1. *Mary, a pet store clerk, sold five trimps and two grimps which have the total of 18 legs. Carlos, another clerk, sold four trimps and three grimps which have the total of 20 legs. How many legs does a trimp have and how many legs does a grimp have?*

KID PIX AS A PROBLEM-SOLVING TOOL

Kid Pix is graphics software for enabling creative activities of young children. Used for more than a decade in educational applications (Chan, 1993), it has been recognized as a tool with potential to support curricula in such areas relatively distant from mathematics as language, geography, and art (Ballenger, 1992). Even an overview of multimedia environments for children that is strongly oriented toward mathematics (Druin & Solomon, 1996) does not mention any mathematical activities with the use of the software. More recently, Brown (1998) argued that the software has potential to be applied across the whole spectrum of the curriculum, yet no specific recommendations were provided in support of the statement.

While many Web sites are available that show mathematical activities for young children that can be enhanced by the use of Kid Pix, traditional print publications on this topic are scarce. Lifter and Adams (1997) recommended using Kid Pix in developing basic counting skills (e.g., counting by twos). Clements (1999) suggested that openness and closeness–the fundamental notions of geometry–can be illustrated through the graphics of Kid Pix. Rosaen, Hobson, and Khan (2003) reported on the use of Kid Pix as an environment for visualizing numbers at the kindergarten level. These uses of the software, though meaningful and important for the mathematical development of young children, fall short of a sophisticated problem-solving context and thus do not reach the level of Type II applications of technology.

In the course of preparing technology-rich materials for a field-based elementary mathematics methods course, I found (Abramovich, 2001) that the use of Kid Pix in the context of Problem 1 by young children has potential to reach the Type II level. Based on this earlier finding, the use of Kid Pix was then extended to include mathematical activities presented through Problems 2.1 and 3.1. To this end, by "editing" custom tools of the software a new set of rubber stamps was created. The new stamps (referred to as *trimps* and *grimps*) represented artificial creatures with a number of legs varying in the one through nine range. Four elementary education students familiar with possible mathematical applications of Kid Pix through the above-mentioned course work were assigned to administer these activities as part of their field work at a small school in rural upstate New York with a group of second-graders chosen from a remedial classroom.

Two 60-minute sessions were conducted in a computer lab. The children were familiar with Kid Pix. However, specific skills such as those related to the use of *trimps* and *grimps* were taught as the activities went along. Two children were paired at the computer, the other two worked individually. In both instances, the children worked on a computer under the tutelage of the pre-teachers and were assisted if they could not perform independently. During the first session, this included guidance in reading and interpreting problems, support in keeping the children's frustration from incorrect guessing at a minimum, help in comprehending the notion of a problem with more than one correct answer (Problem 1), and assistance in recalling conditions of a particular problem when the solution created on a computer screen did not satisfy these conditions.

For the second session, a new set of three problems with different numerical data was created. The goal of the second session was to assure that tutoring during the first session, in which children's problem-solving activities were strongly guided, would not result in dependence on the tutor (Bruner, 1964). Thus, assistance in problem solving during the second session was reduced to a minimum. For example, a need for assistance that occurred during the second session dealt with the children's constructing a solution that was based upon data of a problem from the first session. During both sessions, all children demonstrated nontrivial, on-task behavior that can be ascribed to both the enjoyable context of "pet store mathematics" and the user-friendly environment of Kid Pix.

DEVELOPING A SYSTEM IN RESOLVING INDETERMINATE PROBLEMATIC SITUATIONS

How do young children solve problems with more than one correct answer using graphics software? How can problem-solving performance at the elementary level and that at the higher level be connected? What role can graphics software like Kid Pix play in providing young children with "*objects of thought* [that] become the basis upon which later mathematical thinking occurs" (Connell, 2001, p. 160, italics in the original)? In analyzing the children's informal problem-solving strategies in an indeterminate problematic situation (i.e., a situation in which there is more than one correct response), these questions are of particular interest.

During the second session, it was observed that after initial confusion with Problem 1 (in which 18 was replaced by 16), the first (correct) combination of animals that the pair of children working in collaboration had constructed included only cats. In developing the combination on the screen of a computer using Kid Pix, a child was counting the cats' legs one by one. Because of the visible sloppiness in counting, he was advised by the partner to count by twos–an earlier known strategy that perhaps was never perceived as a problem-solving tool by the children. When he successfully completed counting, the partner uttered, "Good boy!" and, taking her turn, affirmed, "I'll use birds this time." Apparently, this intuitive strategy was prompted by the image of the cats on the computer screen and it resulted from the use of Kid Pix as a recording medium. The strategy was not taught during the first session, and it emerged due to the children's intellectual growth that occurred through problem-solving activities.

The analysis of this strategy indicates the presence of rudiments of advanced mathematical thinking in the children's intuitive approach to finding solutions to what in formal terms is a linear indeterminate equation in two variables. Indeed, this approach parallels a formal (geometric) method of solving such an equation in whole numbers that begins with finding two specific points that belong to its graph; namely, the points of concurrency of the graph with the coordinate axes (points with no birds belong to the cats' axis, points with no cats belong to the birds' axis). To complete the solution, one has to find all lattice points that reside on the segment connecting the two points. Such a search for the lattice points can be recognized in the children's suggestions to each other: "Use more cats!" or "Use more birds!" As a result, all combinations of animals (five in the case of the total of 16 legs) were constructed.

This example shows how the emergence of systematic thinking can be found in young children's intuitive strategies and how those strategies can be identified with more advanced lines of reasoning in a formalized context of solving indeterminate equations. It confirms observations by many researchers that young children are capable of powerful mathematical reasoning manifested through their seemingly naive actions upon developmentally appropriate objects of thought (Connell, 2001). Encouraging young children's informal mathematics in a problem-solving situation can help their intuitive thoughts to develop into a formal realization at the secondary level. Yet, revealing these mathematically rich manifestations of intuitive thinking by the children is not an easy task for elementary pre-teachers. Thus, in the context of teacher education, this study can be used to help pre-teachers understand mathematical thinking of young children.

Another episode worth noting is an attempt to advance the strategy of counting by twos to a higher cognitive plane. More specifically, an apparent success in using this strategy as a tool was a turning point. The child developed an insight that led him to inquire: "*How do we count by fours?*" It is clear that counting by fours represents an operation that second-graders were not familiar with; however, such an operation, when mediated by enjoyable context and tools that encourage playful thinking, was developmentally appropriate. In other words, the concept of counting by fours belonged to the child's "zone of proximal development" (Vygotsky, 1978)–a dynamic characteristic of cognition that, in a problem-solving situation, measures the distance between two levels of the child's development as determined by independent and assisted performances. The ability to ask questions indicates one's readiness to go beyond the actual level of development based on earlier experiences with the help of another, more knowledgeable person. Apparently, "[b]y asking a question, the child indicates that he has, in fact, formulated a plan to solve the task before him, but is unable to perform all the necessary operations" (Vygotsky, p. 29). Although assistance in counting by fours was not provided at that point, had it occurred, it could have been described as assisted performance at those points of the zone where assistance is required. Note that such an assistance is what Tharp and Gallimore (1988) have conceptualized as teaching. Overall, this episode shows how learning to perform higher cognitive functions can be motivated by Type II applications of technology.

DEVELOPING SKILLS IN USING ALGEBRAIC SYMBOLISM

Another interesting finding that resulted from this study is the ability of second-graders to move with relative ease from representing a problematic situation through graphics (iconic representation) to its representation through written symbols. The traditional approach to applied algebra problem solving is to start with writing equations (mathematical models) and continue with solving these equations using strictly defined rules of mathematics. Such an approach is not possible until higher grades. Furthermore, the grasp of the deductive structure of moving from general to specific (i.e., from an algebraic equation to its numeric solution) is often extremely difficult for learners to follow because of the technical complexity of the correct application of mathematical rules. In the context of Problems 2.1 and 3.1, children were moving in the opposite direction by being led into the use of symbolism through drawing. A question to be answered in this section is: How was that achieved?

To this end, note that one can distinguish, using Vygotsky's (1978) terminology, the introduction of "first-order symbols . . . directly denoting objects of actions, . . . [from] . . . second-order symbolism, which involves the creation of written signs for the spoken symbols of words . . . [and] develops [by] shifting from drawing of things to drawing of words" (p. 115). Indeed, whereas variables were introduced to children as first-order symbols–a notation that reflects quantity associated with objects of their actions, equations that relate these variables to each other were introduced as second-order symbols–a notation that reflects relationships among the quantified objects. Kid Pix, or any graphics software, provides young children with tools capable of making a shift from using first-order symbols to acquiring second-order symbolism. It is through meaningful play that children can move from creating graphics-based solutions of problematic situations to writing true algebraic equations (mathematical sentences) that rigorously model the situations. A practical implication of the approach of teaching second-order symbolism through play is that it can be done earlier than usual–a recommendation by Vygotsky (1978) for the teaching of writing. Such a recommendation can be extended to other school subjects, including algebra. Indeed, the construction of equations as symbolic representations of concrete situations can be introduced early in mathematics education provided that appropriate computer tools, like graphics software, can accommodate children's move from drawing objects of actions to drawing symbolic relations that quantitatively describe these objects.

The use of Kid Pix enables young children to develop functions of both first- and second-order symbolism by using "talking" letters and numerals as elements in a support system. The success in developing these functions by the children using Kid Pix can be explained in terms of the "method of double stimulation" (Vygotsky, 1962, p. 56). Indeed, one can note that in the course of moving from icons to symbols, two sets of stimuli were involved: The first set included rubber stamps of letters/numerals as objects of the children's activity, and the second set included verbal representations of the stamps that were employed to mediate the activity. "Talking" letters/numerals represent a sign system that served as an enhancement of young children's internal speech.

Thus, in the mediated process of writing mathematical sentences, "the child is able to include stimuli that do not lie within the immediate visual field" (Vygotsky, 1978, p. 26). In this, Vygotsky insisted on the importance of semiotic mediation (i.e., mediation by artifacts) in the development of human consciousness.

As an illustration, consider the problem-solving context of Problem 3.1. It was found that a second-grader from a remedial classroom was capable of implicitly solving a system of simultaneous equations "via actions upon developmentally appropriate objects" (Connell, 2001, p. 161) and then explicitly representing this system through the use of meaningful (to her) symbols *T* and *G* associated with artificial creatures *trimps* and *grimps*. The trial-and-error approach, which was not directly taught to the children but rather emerged as an intuitive problem-solving strategy, enabled the child, in fact, to solve the system of equations as a physical activity by partitioning 18 objects into five groups with one cardinality and two groups with another cardinality and then, using the same grouping principle, partitioning 20 objects into four and three such groups. This partitioning perspective may be considered a method of solving systems of two simultaneous equations in whole numbers, something that is not commonly taught even at the secondary level. In such a way, a partitioning problem-solving strategy developed with the help of graphics software can be adapted as a formal method for solving high school algebra problems.

To conclude this section, note that, despite overall success in resolving the partitioning brainteaser, a challenge for the child was to recognize the fact that, if the first partition is a correct one, then the second partition should not involve trial and error but rather a check-in strategy. More specifically, if from the pictorial representation of the partitioning of 18 legs, it follows that a *trimp* has two legs and a *grimp* has four legs, one may develop the second combination of creatures by testing whether four and three such *trimps* and *grimps*, respectively, give the total of 20 legs. This kind of reasoning, however, has not been observed; apparently it was beyond the ability of the child.

CONCLUSION

The use of graphics software in the context of activities described in this paper enabled multiple pedagogical ideas to be used. One such idea was to demonstrate that graphics software is an appropriate tool for enhancing early algebra curriculum. In the last two decades, many authors focused on the role that *graphing* software could play in the teaching and learning of algebra. In particular, Kaput (1989) anticipated significant changes in what it means to solve an equation as a result of using such technology. As this paper has described, a meaningful change can emerge from the appropriate use of *graphics* software also. While computers could not and should not replace students' abilities to solve algebraic equations in a traditional way (i.e., through the use of formal rules of algebra), exploring "new ways of thinking about actions on equations" (Kaput, p. 181) at the elementary level has potential to raise cognitive abilities of young children to higher ground. Furthermore, through the use of graphics software, several informal problem-solving skills that can be adapted at the secondary level can naturally develop.

Another pedagogical idea behind the activities was to show pre-service teachers (participating as tutors) how to orient computer-mediated instruction to enhance the development of residual mental power (i.e., something that remains in the mind when a support system is removed) in young children that can be used in the absence of a tutor. In general, the goal of such pedagogy is to ensure that today's collaboration with a more knowledgeable other could result in a zone of proximal development and thus would facilitate an independent performance tomorrow (Vygotsky, 1987). As Berg (1970) noted, although Vygotsky did not make clear how instruction could use the zone of proximal development, "he would perhaps recommend that teachers and pupils work together to solve problems and to do activities that pupils couldn't do by themselves. The teachers' job would be to provide cues and clues to help the pupil over hurdles he couldn't get over himself" (p. 385). It is precisely this kind of pedagogy that was learned first hand by pre-teachers through their practicum.

It should be noted that the described use of graphics software as a tool for doing mathematics made it possible to substitute computer-mediated tasks for algebraic tasks so that for those commonly struggling with mathematics, the unity of content and pedagogy was particularly advantageous. This pedagogical approach brings about a qualitative change in a learning process through the use of computers, and thus it represents a clear-cut example of a Type II application of technology. As this paper has demonstrated, by using various tools and features included in an expanded software repertoire, young children were able to represent mathematical situations at different levels of sophistication and grow intellectually as activities went along. The fact that the children were able to self-structure and–most importantly–goal-organize their problem-solving activities while mediating them by tools and signs of the software, is a testimony to their intellectual growth (Berg, 1970). I believe that such growth is due to pedagogy that introduces early algebra into a mathematics classroom, and thus enhances tomorrow's development of these young children.

REFERENCES

Abramovich, S. (2001). Cultural tools and mathematics teacher education. In F. R. Curcio (Ed.), *Proceedings of the Third U.S.-Russia Joint Conference on Mathematics Education and the Mathematics Education Seminar at the University of Goteborg* (pp. 61-67). Spokane, WA: People to People Ambassador Programs.

Ballenger, M. (1992). Software for the classroom. *Childhood Education, 69*(2), 118-119.

Berg, E. E. (1970). *L. S. Vygotsky's theory of the social and historical origins of consciousness* (Dissertation). Ann Arbor, MI: University Microfilms, Inc.

Broderbund Software, Inc. (2001). *KidPix® Deluxe 3™ [Computer software].* Novato, CA: Author.

Brown, C. A. (1998). Presentation software and the single computer. *Learning and Leading with Technology, 26*(2), 18-21.

Bruner, J. S. (1964). Some theorems on instruction illustrated with reference to mathematics. In E. R. Hilgard (Ed.), *Theories of learning and instructions* (pp. 306-335). Chicago: The National Society for the Study of Education.

Chan, B. J. (1993). *Kid Pix around the world.* Reading, MA: Addison Wesley.

Clements, D. H. (1999). The effective use of computers with young children. In J. V. Copley (Ed.), *Mathematics in the early years* (pp. 119-128). Reston, VA: National Council of Teachers of Mathematics.

Connell, M. (2001). Actions on objects: A metaphor for technology-enhanced mathematics instruction. *Computers in the Schools, 17*(1/2), 143-171.

Dienes, Z. (1960). *Building up mathematics.* London: Hutchinson.

Druin, A., & Solomon, C. (1996). *Designing multimedia environments for children.* New York: Wiley.

Jonassen, D. H. (1996). *Computers in the classroom: Mindtools for critical thinking.* Englewood Cliffs, NJ: Prentice-Hall.

Kaput, J. J. (1989). Linking representations in the symbol systems of algebra. In S. Wagner & C. Kieran (Eds.), *Research issues in the learning and teaching of algebra* (pp. 167-194). Reston, VA: National Council of Teachers of Mathematics.

Lifter, M., & Adams, M. E. (1997). *Kid Pix for terrified teachers.* Huntington Beach, CA: Teacher Created Materials, Inc.

Maddux, C. D. (1994). Editorial: Integration is the only option we have. *Journal of Information Technology for Teacher Education, 3*(2), 129-133.

Maddux, C. D., Johnson, D. L., & Willis, J. W. (1997). *Educational computing: Learning with tomorrow's technologies.* Boston: Allyn & Bacon.

Means, B. (1994). Introduction: Using technology to advance educational goals. In B. Means (Ed.), *Technology and education reform* (pp. 1-21). San Francisco: Jossey-Bass.

National Council of Teachers of Mathematics. (1989). *Curriculum and evaluation standards for school mathematics.* Reston, VA: Author.

National Council of Teachers of Mathematics. (2000). *Principles and standards for school mathematics.* Reston, VA: Author.

New York State Education Department. (1998). *Mathematics resource guide with core curriculum.* Albany, NY: Author.

Rosaen, C. L., Hobson, S., & Khan, G. (2003). Making connections: Collaborative approaches to preparing today's and tomorrow's teachers to use technology. *Journal of Technology and Teacher Education, 11*(2), 281-306.

Tharp, R. G., & Gallimore, R. (1988). *Rousing minds to life: Teaching, learning, and schooling in social context.* Cambridge: Cambridge University Press.

Vygotsky, L. S. (1962). *Thought and language.* Cambridge, MA: The MIT Press.

Vygotsky, L. S. (1978). *Mind in society.* Cambridge, MA: Harvard University.

Vygotsky, L. S. (1987). Thinking and speech. In R. W. Rieber & A. S. Carton (Eds.), *The collected works of L. S. Vygotsky* (vol. 1, pp. 39-285). New York: Plenum Press.

Maryanne R. Bednar
John J. Sweeder

Defining and Applying Idea Technologies: A Systematic, Conceptual Framework for Teachers

SUMMARY. In this paper we define and explain idea technologies, illustrate how they operate in learning environments, then present and explore the pedagogical advantages of using our three-tiered, idea-technology classification system. We believe it will serve as an introductory primer, or conceptual framework, for university professors, educational technologists, teacher educators, and university administrators. Like any sound grammar, we believe our conceptual framework not only provides structure, economy, and flexibility, but also possesses the added benefit of never "crashing" as it improves teaching and learning. *[Article copies available for a fee from The Haworth Document Delivery Service: 1-800-HAWORTH. E-mail address: <docdelivery@haworthpress.com> Website: <http://www.HaworthPress.com> © 2005 by The Haworth Press, Inc. All rights reserved.]*

KEYWORDS. Educational technology, teacher education, Type II technology application, pedagogy, idea-technology classification, Idea Technologies Matrix

MARYANNE R. BEDNAR is Associate Professor, Department of Education, La Salle University, Philadelphia, PA 19141 (E-mail: bednar@lasalle.edu).
JOHN J. SWEEDER is Associate Professor, Department of Education, La Salle University, Philadelphia, PA 19141 (E-mail: sweeder@lasalle.edu).

[Haworth co-indexing entry note]: "Defining and Applying Idea Technologies: A Systematic, Conceptual Framework for Teachers." Bednar, Maryanne R., and John J. Sweeder. Co-published simultaneously in *Computers in the Schools* (The Haworth Press, Inc.) Vol. 22, No. 3/4, 2005, pp. 35-47; and: *Classroom Integration of Type II Uses of Technology in Education* (ed: Cleborne D. Maddux, and D. LaMont Johnson) The Haworth Press, Inc., 2005, pp. 35-47. Single or multiple copies of this article are available for a fee from The Haworth Document Delivery Service [1-800-HAWORTH, 9:00 a.m. - 5:00 p.m. (EST). E-mail address: docdelivery@haworthpress.com].

Available online at http://www.haworthpress.com/web/CITS

doi:10.1300/J025v22n03_04

Teachers' reluctance to incorporate educational technology into their classroom instruction may occur for a variety of reasons, including lack of technical and administrative support staff, potential embarrassment of looking inept in front of students, and a belief that technology does not really help achieve instructional goals (Zhao & Cziko, 2001). For teachers to incorporate technology effectively into their classroom instruction, they need to perceive its utility and power. In order to do this, they must first fully understand what *educational technology* is and discover ways in which they may already be using it. When such a foundation is established, teachers will gain confidence, be more likely to employ it again, and become more willing to let their students use it as well. As shown in Figure 1, educational technology is the systematic and creative blending of product and idea technologies (Hooper & Rieber, 1995) in order to engender teaching and learning within and/or across subject-matter disciplines (Sweeder & Bednar, 2001; Sweeder, Bednar, & Ryan, 1998).

When discussions of integrating educational technology into the classroom occur, the emphasis is often attributed to "cutting-edge" product technologies–particularly high-tech digital hardware such as high-speed multimedia computers, personal digital assistants, tablet PCs, and wireless laptops that connect to the Internet. Subsequently, idea technologies, defined as theoretical yet practical cognitive schemata that act as blueprints to explain and operationalize abstractions (Ryan, Bednar, & Sweeder, 1999, p. 119), receive short shrift because they are less tangible, more tacit. Examples of idea technologies include multiple intelligence theory, WebQuests, and the writing process. We suspect that when teachers become fully cognizant of the direct relationship between powerful idea technologies and their subject matter content, active intellectual involvement of teachers and learners occurs in creative, interactive, and innovative ways, not unlike what occurs with Maddux, Johnson, and Willis's (2001) Type II technology application characteristics: user intellectual involvement, interactive user control, the accomplishment of creative tasks, and many hours of user experience in mastering software (pp. 119-120). Although Type II applications reference computer software exclusively, idea technologies, on the other hand, include not only computer software, but also a wide range of cognitive schemata (see Table 1).

The purpose of the present paper is to define and explain what idea technologies are and illustrate how they operate in learning environments as well as present and explore the advantages of using our idea-technology classification system. It is our belief that educators

FIGURE 1. Educational technology: The creative and systematic blending of idea and product technologies with subject-matter content.

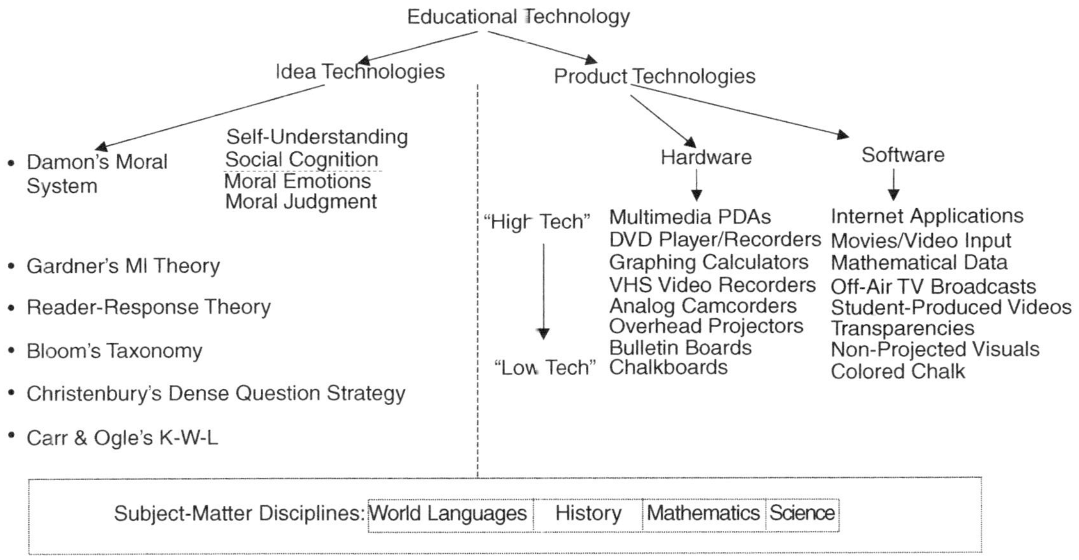

TABLE 1. Idea Technologies Matrix: Core, Mantle, and Crust Idea Technology Examples

Core Idea Technologies Tier One	Mantle Idea Technologies Tier Two	Crust Idea Technologies Tier Three
• Piaget's Theory of Cognitive Development • Gardner's Multiple Intelligence Theory • Sternberg's Multiple Intelligence Theory • Kohlberg's Theory of Moral Development • Gilligan's Ethic of Care • Goleman's Emotional Intelligence • Damon's Moral System • Wilson's Moral Sentiments • Selman's Perspective-Taking Theory • Gregorc's Learning Styles Theory • Erikson's Theory of Psycho-Social Development • Marcia's Identity Statuses • Helm's Model of Ethnic Idea Development • Vygotsky's Social-Constructivist Theory of Social Development • Skinner's Operant Conditioning • Information Processing Theory • Freud's Theory of Psychosexual Development • Bandura's Observational Learning • Meichenbaum's Cognitive Behavioral Modification	• Bloom's Taxonomy of Cognitive Objectives • Ogle and Carr's K-W-L-Plus • Gardner's Entry Points • Stauffer's Direct Reading Thinking Activity (D-R-T-A) and Bednar's variations: Directed Music Thinking Activity (D-M-T-A) and Directed Video Thinking Activity (D-V-T-A) • Scientific Method • Flower and Hayes's Writing Process • Dodge's and Marsh's WebQuest • Robinson's SQ3R and variations thereof SQ4R, and PQ4R • Stauffer's Language Experience Approach (LEA) • McTingue and Lyman Think-Pair-Share • Hyerle's Visual Tools • Wilen et al.'s Questioning-Circle System • Bednar's Strategic Reading Model (SRM) • Problem-Based Learning • Rosenblatt's Reader Response Theory • Johnson et al.'s Cooperative Learning Principles • Dales's Cone of Experience • Harris's Tele-Computing Activities • Bruner's Modes of Representation of Knowledge/Discovery Learning Approach • Sherman's Videographing Process • Chiappetta, Koballa, & Collette's Inductive Laboratory	English/Languages • Burke's Notes & Quotes • Burke's Dense Questioning System • Benson's Essay Question Format History and Social Studies • Fling's Historical Method • Sweeder's "Who Dreamed" narrational entry • Allen and Stevens's "Protect that Source: A Mock Trial" Mathematics • Ryan et al.'s "A Calculated Decision" lesson plan • FOIL method for multiplying binomials • Holmes's "Growing, Growing, Graphing" Science • Latham's "Animating Motion" lesson plan • Ryan et al.'s "Peas in a Pod" lesson plan • De Prisco-Havasy and Patysiak's "Pendulums on the Moon" lesson plan Reading • Beck et al.'s Question the Author (QTA) • Hobbs's Media Literacy Activity • Bednar's Text Tags

should apprehend, apply, and blend *idea* technologies, just as they do *product* technologies in order to reach more of the students more of the time.

IDEA TECHNOLOGIES: CORE, MANTLE, AND CRUST

Idea technologies foster effective teaching and learning. Our conceptual framework addresses professional knowledge (i.e., a body of content that classroom teachers need to know) and takes into consideration the varied needs of learners (e.g., heterogeneous small groups of adolescents) as well as the subject matter content being taught. Similar to the Earth itself, idea technologies consist of three, interrelated layers: the core, mantle, and crust.

Core idea technologies are conceptually robust in that they provide teachers with far-reaching and central understanding of human behaviors that are found across cultures, time, and space. Erikson's theory of psychosocial development (Santrock, 2003), Gardner's multiple intelligence theory (1999), and Damon's moral system (Ryan, Sweeder, & Bednar, 2002) are examples of core idea technologies. Core idea technologies are comprehensive in that they help educators of all walks of life more fully understand how individuals think and learn.

To illustrate how core idea technologies operate, let us examine Erikson's eight-stage theory of psychosocial development. He posits that human beings across all cultures encounter and resolve, successfully or unsuccessfully, several developmental crises. If infants receive timely amounts of love, care, shelter, and nourishment during the first year of their lives, they will likely develop trusting personalities and become ready to move on to the second stage: autonomy versus shame and doubt. If, however, they do not, they will become distrustful (as well as fixated), and thus may find it difficult to advance to the next phase of their development. Since teachers of students are aware of this, they readily recognize that if some students in their classes are not "ready" to learn because they lack confidence, initiative, and a sense of industry, teachers may need to first establish a trusting relationship with their learners.

A philosophically different foundational idea technology, Gardner's multiple intelligence theory, suggests that each human being possesses a unique set of eight cognitive capabilities that comprise his or her intelligence profile (D'Arcangelo, 1997). In Western society, linguistic and mathematical/logical intelligences traditionally have been valued more highly. However, other cultures may hold spatial, naturalistic, and interpersonal intelligences in higher regard. Since 21st century school populations are increasingly diverse, and increasingly greater numbers of teachers recognize that students do not necessarily think and learn alike, students' intellectual profiles may differ. Thus, Gardner's theory provides a conceptual framework teachers can rely upon for support as they devise lesson plans, activities, and assessments.

Second-layer or *mantle idea technologies* emanate from and build upon core idea technologies. They are more directly related to the educational enterprise in that they usually serve as pedagogical "rules of thumb." As such, they provide baseline professional knowledge for pre-service, novice, and experienced teachers. Second-layer idea technologies transcend academic disciplines or specific subject matter content and, in some respects, are similar to Shulman's (1987) concept of "general pedagogical knowledge" (p. 8). Examples of second-layer idea technologies include cognitive mapping and visual tools (Hyerle, 1996), Sherman's three-stage videographic process (1991), and the writing process (Flower, 1981).

To illustrate the point, let us examine the question-circle system (QCS) (Christenbury & Kelly, 1983), which we classify as a layer-two idea technology. Intended initially as a framework for secondary English teachers, the QCS enables classroom instructors of *any* discipline to systematically author and orchestrate reflective discussions that help students address three separate, yet overlapping and intersecting domains: one's personal reality, one's external reality, and the specific text being studied. Using these three domains, teachers can craft up to seven increasingly "dense" questions (Burke, 1999) intended to engender lively interactive, classroom discussion as well as provoke deeper, higher level thinking. Another example of a tier-two idea technology is Dodge and Marsh's (2003) WebQuest. Basically, WebQuests structure students' Internet searches and make them more productive and fun. Typically, WebQuests provide creative entrées into content-area investigations by using the following components: an introduction that stimulates students' problem-solving abilities; a specific task to accomplish; a designated process; print, human and "teacher-approved" electronic resources or pathways; an evaluation, which often includes a rubric; and conclusion, whereby students receive appropriate feedback (visit http://webquest.sdsu.edu/).

Crust technologies provide everyday classroom teachers with specific tactics to help students master particular subject matter content in more efficient and/or engaging ways. Crust technologies may find their nascence *from* and *within* mantle and/or core technologies (such as Bloom's taxonomy or Gardner's multiple intelligence theory) when teachers operationalize first- and/or second-tier technologies in order *to address specific subject matter content in a particular discipline*; thus, the process is a deductive one. Other times, the genesis of crust technologies occurs when classroom teachers problem solve in order *to create precise steps or unique, creative examples* that they can use to help learners master specific subject matter content or illuminate new, challenging, or abstract concepts. And so, this is more of an intuitive, inductive process. Still, there are other crust technologies that are transducive in nature and are manifested as *a blend of the aforementioned inductive and deductive processes*. Viewed as a whole, third-tier idea technologies resemble Shulman's pedagogical content knowledge (1987), "the blending of content and pedagogy into an understanding of how particular topics, problems, or issues are organized, represented, and adapted to the diverse interests and abilities of learners and presented for instruction" (p. 8).

Some examples of crust technologies that are *derived from second-tier mantle technologies* include the Directed Reading Thinking Activity (D-R-T-A) (Stauffer, 1969) and the K-W-L-Plus design (Carr & Ogle, 1987), each of which provides a framework for teaching or learning about any subject matter discipline. For instance, when a secondary high school English teacher recognizes that her learners are struggling with Swift's "A Modest Proposal," she may *deliberately* adjust the D-R-T-A by providing additional background knowledge, deconstructing the text into more manageable chunks or segments, and subsequently, elucidating specific purposes for each of the text's segments, in order for her students to become more comfortable with the language, sentence structure, literary convention, and thematic points.

Similarly, Ogle and Carr's K-W-L-Plus design provides a second-tier, mantle-level technology that transforms into a crust technology when secondary teachers *intentionally* apply its basic framework to address a specific subject matter topic in order to meet the needs of a particular student demographic. For instance, when a high school teacher creates a set induction for her American history unit entitled *Manifest Destiny*, he employs the first step of the K-W-L-Plus, "K" or "What do I already know?" by asking students to brainstorm all the information that they know, or believe that they know, about the American westward movement period, 1865-1900. This, then, becomes the springboard for clarifying issues and misconceptions when the teacher acts as a scaffold in guiding students as they form their own questions for further investigation: "W" or "What do I need to know?" Finally, after students have read the text, viewed films, and conducted Internet searches for primary documents, the class fuses the pre-existing information with the new information to understand that American westward expansion is but one example of the concept *Manifest Destiny*, completing the "L" or "What I have learned." Students finally conduct individual research looking for other examples of *Manifest Destiny*, thus operationalizing the Plus component of the K-W-L.

Benson (1991), in response to her desire to have her students learn successfully how to take challenging, end-of-year essay exams in her secondary English classes, invents a tier-three idea technology. Believing that writing itself is one on the best ways for students to connect prior knowledge to new learning, she creates and subsequently teaches her students how to answer essay-test questions, using a unique, idiosyncratic format. She describes four overlapping yet distinctive types of essay questions–factual, document-based, creative and evaluative–that she administers to her learners, in order to determine how well they have mastered a particular body of knowledge, such as a play that they read. This is a year-long, developmental process whereby she takes the time, after administering each test, to review how each student essay is assessed by breaking each essay question down into its component parts.

Likewise, Sweeder (Sweeder, Bednar, & Ryan, 1997) explains that, as he prepares for his undergraduate-level Educational Psychology I course, he invents an engaging entry to a mini-unit on Freud's psychosexual theory. He begins his lesson with one simple question: Who dreamed last night? After his students share their dreams, he shares one of his own, which deals with his preternatural ability to fly. Probing individual students by asking them what they think the people, places, events, and objects in their dreams might mean or symbolize, he moves the lecture forward by explaining how dream analysis is just one of the tools of the psychoanalyst, a tool Freud himself used. The lecture proceeds in a logical, linear progression as Sweeder explains Freud's three personality structures, varied states of consciousness, and five stages of psychosexual development.

Blended crust technologies sometimes occur through trial and error, but more often than not they originate through reflective practice engendered by reading the professional literature and/or through discussions with colleagues. Examples might include: Text Tags for secondary-level learners (Bednar, 2004), a blending of reader-response theory (Rosenblatt, 1994) and an adaptation of Sticky-Note

Reading (Cunningham & Allington, 1999), and Latham's blending of Inductive Laboratory (Chiappetta, Koballa, & Collette, 1998) and his own creative energy to create a series of crust-level technologies, Animating Motion (<http://school.discovery.com/lessonplans/activities/animatingmotion/>).

When teaching the concept of *voice*, high school English teachers often experience difficulty in getting their adolescents to understand better how voice is related to the three interrelated concepts: *mood*, *tone* and *diction*. To illuminate how an author conveys voice through mood, tone, and diction, a high school English teacher might choose to apply Text Tags, a third-tier idea technology whereby the teacher gives students different colored post-it notes™ to make notations as they read. In this case, students are instructed to place *yellow* post-its notes™ directly upon those portions of the novel where they have determined that the writer's tone has been conveyed through his or her word choice. Students use *blue* post-it notes™ when they, as readers, respond personally to passages in the text that elicit within them a particular affect (e.g., fear) that may or may not be the response intended by the author or the teacher. By incorporating color-coded post-it notes™, the teacher and the students reference specific textual evidence, which they subsequently use to support or challenge one another's understanding of how the novelist's voice proceeds directly from his or her tone and diction–as well as its possible influence on the reader's mood. In summary, the purpose of using Text Tags is to convey to the students the fact that a *subtle* interplay often exists between tone and mood.

Latham's Animating Motion is another blended crust technology (<http://school.discovery.com/lessonplans/activities/animatingmotion/>) that adapts the Inductive Laboratory (Chiappetta, Koballa, & Collette, 1998) approach in order to provide an effective physics lesson that explores the concept of *object motion*. Through a sequence of three online Web "Challenges" students apply their prior knowledge (initially provided in the "Background" section of Latham's Web page) by animating the orbital motions of the Earth, the motion of a falling object, and the motion of a car, truck, and plane. By briefly explaining what *kinematics* is and by supplying specific formulae to express quantitatively an object's motion, Latham guides students as they practice graphing and animating the motion of objects.

As a subgroup, crust technologies are tactical, in contrast to mantle and core technologies, which are more conceptual and/or strategic in nature. Crust technologies hold strong appeal because of their concrete, immediate, and utilitarian nature: Teachers often employ them in their daily lesson plans. Crust technologies, however, should not be mistaken as mere "tricks of the trade" or "short-term fixes" that enable teachers to engage and entertain students for a 50- or 90-minute class period; used as such, crust technologies become "fool's gold" in that their potency diminishes whenever teachers apply them mechanistically or overuse them. Whether they emanate directly from mantle or core technologies, or surface in direct response to learning issues witnessed in individual classrooms, crust technologies provide a coherent, pedagogical foundation for teaching and learning.

IDEA TECHNOLOGIES MATRIX

In our view, effective teachers blend idea technologies from all levels–core, mantle, and crust–in coherent, challenging, and novel ways to engage their learners, help them master new knowledge, and develop as human beings. When students experience teaching and learning grounded in a coherent philosophy (i.e., a unifying thread connecting all three layers of idea technologies), they begin to recognize–either tacitly or consciously–that classroom instruction contains a sense of *past* (a history, if you will), *present* (the objectives for today's lesson), and *future* (or where they are headed); thus, an overarching structure becomes artfully blended with content. To more easily apprehend our conceptual model, consider the following Idea Technologies Matrix (see Table 1). Recognizing the fact that teachers can use this matrix in different ways–deductively, inductively, or transactively–they may choose to incorporate three separate idea technologies–a core, a mantle, and a crust–in order to create a course of study, a unit of instruction, or even a single lesson plan. For instance, when a geography teacher wants her urban middle schoolers to master the names of North America's five Great Lakes: Huron, Ontario, Michigan, Erie, and Superior, she introduces the mnemonic, HOMES, a word that carries meaning for her learners. Notwithstanding the fact that her instructional objective is a modest one (i.e., simple recall), her use of idea technologies might be quite sophisticated and effective. Devising an acronym to master specific content is a form of crust idea technology, which in turn, is embedded in the more general mantle technology of mnemonics themselves, in which teachers and learners "chunk" new bits of unrelated information or data in such a way as to facilitate later recall. Such mantle memory devices are further embedded in the core or foundational idea technology of information processing theory.

Hobbs (2001) describes a more elaborate blending of core, mantle and crust idea technologies in Helen Rochester's (as cited in Hobbs, 2001, pp. 46-48) engaging *Assignment: Media Literacy* curriculum. To help middle school reluctant readers understand what effective *character development* is and how authors achieve it, Rochester utilizes a crust technology tailored to her specific learners' needs, the character wheel, which is a subject-specific form of graphic organizer, a mantle technology. Then, by further blending Slavin's jigsaw cooperative learning approach (as cited in Wilen, Bosse, Hutchison, & Kindsvatter, 2004, pp. 299-300)–another mantle technology–with Presseley's *transactional strategies instruction* (as cited in Hobbs, 2001, p. 47), she divides her students into six coteries, holding each responsible for mastering and teaching one another the content of each component of the character wheel: thoughts, physical appearance, reactions of others, speech/dialogue, behavior/actions, and setting. Rochester draws from Vygotsky's social constructivist theory (Woolfolk, 2001) as well as Selman's perspective-taking stage theory (Santrock, 2003) when her students use video clips and classroom dialogues to assert, challenge, and change their perspectives of their assigned character's behavior, thoughts, reactions, etc., depicted on their group's character wheel.

MATRIX: PEDAGOGICAL AND RESEARCH APPLICATIONS

The Idea Technologies Matrix can be used in a variety of productive ways: as a primer, point of departure, assessment device, mentoring tool, and springboard to refining or challenging the model itself. The matrix serves as an introductory primer educators can use in creative and systematic ways. Useful as a handy reference when planning a lesson, unit, or course, the Idea Technologies Matrix presents an array (albeit an incomplete one) of theoretically sound, literature-based frameworks that provide structure, cohesion, and vitality to classroom instruction.

Teacher educators may introduce the idea technology matrix to their students so that these pre-service teachers are better able to understand in an efficient manner, some specific pedagogical choices they have at their convenience. Principals, media specialists, and educational technologists will find that the Idea Technologies Matrix provides them with an innovative mentoring tool to use with in-service teachers. In many schools, access to cutting-edge, high tech product technology is either impractical or next to impossible. Nevertheless, school leaders might initiate stimulating faculty workshops by distributing the matrix for teachers to discover collaboratively creative, yet systematic ways in which they can blend core, mantle, and crust technologies with whatever instructional hardware and software their schools already possess. Educators may choose to use this matrix as a gauge in order to assess their own knowledge and use of idea technologies. Depending upon his or her own self-analysis, a teacher might consider engaging in additional formal or informal study to build a more extensive knowledge base about a particular core, mantle, or crust technology. Alternatively, educational researchers might find the matrix a catalyst for further academic investigation. Educators should apprehend, apply, and blend *idea* technologies, just as they do *product* technologies.

REFERENCES

Bednar, M. (2004, March). Idea technology and product technology: Seeing beyond the text to the technology that works. *Voices from the Middle, 11*(3), 34-37.

Benson, B. (1991). Effective tests: Let them write! *English Journal, 80*(3), 74-79.

Burke, J. (1999). *The English teacher's companion.* Portsmouth, NH: Boynton/Cook.

Carr, E., & Ogle, C.M. (1987). K-W-L-Plus: A strategy in comprehension and summarization. *Journal of Reading, 30,* 626-631.

Chiappetta, E. L., Koballa, Jr., T. R., & Collette, A. T. (1998). *Science instruction in the middle and secondary schools* (4th ed.). Upper Saddle River, NJ: Merrill.

Christenbury, L., & Kelly, P. (1983). *Questioning: A path to critical thinking.* Urbana, IL: ERIC Clearinghouse on Reading and Communication Skills and the National Council of Teachers of English. (ERIC Document Reproduction Service No. ED226372)

Cunningham, P. M., & Allington, R. L. (1999). *Classrooms that work* (2nd ed.). New York: Longman.

D'Arcangelo, M. (Project Manager and Producer). (1997). *Exploring our multiple intelligences* [CD-ROM]. Alexandria, VA: Association for Supervision and Curriculum Development. (Stock No. 59276)

Dodge, B., & Marsh, T. *TheWebQuest page.* Retrieved February 14, 2003, from http://webquest.sdsu.edu/

Flower, L. (1981). *Problem-solving strategies for writing.* New York: Harcourt Brace Jovanovich.

Gardner, H. (1999). *Intelligence reframed: Multiple intelligences for the 21st century.* New York: Basic Books.

Hobbs, R. (2001). Improving reading comprehension by using media literacy activities. *Voices from the Middle, 8*(4), 44-50.

Hooper, S., & Rieber, L. (1995). Teaching with technology. In A. Ornstein (Ed.), *Teaching: Theory into practice* (pp. 154-170). Needham Heights, MA: Allyn & Bacon.

Hyerle, D. (1996). *Visual tools for constructing knowledge*. Alexandria, VA: Association for Supervision and Curriculum Development.
Maddux, C., Johnson, D., & Willis, J. (2001). *Educational computing: Learning with tomorrow's technologies* (3rd ed.). Boston, MA: Allyn & Bacon.
Rosenblatt, L. (1994). The transactional theory of reading and writing. In R. B. Ruddell, M. R. Ruddell, & H. Singer (Eds.), *Theoretical models and processing of reading* (4th ed., pp. 1057-1092). Newark, DE: International Reading Association.
Ryan, F. J., Bednar, M. R., & Sweeder, J. J. (1999). Technology, narcissism, and the moral sense: Implications for instruction. *British Journal of Educational Technology, 30*(2), 115-128.
Ryan, F. J., Sweeder, J. J., & Bednar, M. R. (2002). *Drowning in the clear pool: Cultural narcissism, technology, and character education*. NY: Peter Lang.
Santrock, J. W. (2003). *Adolescence* (9th ed.). Boston, MA: McGraw-Hill.
Sherman, M. (1991). *Videographing the pictorial sequence*. Washington, DC: Association for Educational Communications and Technology.
Shulman, L. (1987). Knowledge and teaching: Foundation of the new reform. *Harvard Educational Review, 57*(1), 1-22.
Stauffer, R. (1969). *Directing reading maturity as a cognitive process*. NY: Harper & Row.
Sweeder, J. J., & Bednar, M. R. (2001). "Flying" with educational technology. *Contemporary Issues in Technology and Teacher Education, 1*(3). Retrieved July 21, 2004, from http://www.citejournal.org/vol1/iss3/currentpractice/article2.htm
Sweeder, J. J., Bednar, M. R., & Ryan, F. J. (1997, April). *Conjoining product technologies with multiple intelligence theory: Rethinking teacher preparation*. Presentation at the Eighth International Conference, Society for Information Technology and Teacher Education, Orlando, FL.
Sweeder, J. J., Bednar, M. R., & Ryan, F. J. (1998). Conjoining product technologies with multiple intelligence theory: Rethinking teacher preparation. *Journal of Technology and Teacher Education, 6*(4), 273-282.
Wilen, W., Bosse, M. I., Hutchison, J., & Kindsvatter, R. (2004). *Dynamics of effective secondary teaching* (5th ed.). Boston, MA: Pearson Education.
Woolfolk, A. (2001). *Educational Psychology* (8th ed.). Boston, MA: Allyn & Bacon.
Zhao, Y., & Cziko, G. A. (2001). Teacher adoption of technology: A perceptual control theory perspective. *Journal of Technology and Teacher Education, 9*(1), 5-30.

Jody S. Britten
Jerrel C. Cassady

The Technology Integration Assessment Instrument: Understanding Planned Use of Technology by Classroom Teachers

SUMMARY. Cognizant of the difficulty teachers face in attempting to integrate computers into instructional settings, the authors propose a new technology integration assessment strategy that can guide individual development or be used to track programmatic change. The Technology Integration Assessment Instrument (TIAI) explores seven dimensions of planning with specific attention to levels of technology integration. Repeated use of the TIAI is anticipated to promote individuals' abilities to track their own growth, as well as provide a standard method for documenting the application of Type II uses of educational computing. This paper presents the TIAI, identifying the method of analyzing lesson plans employed in this system, as well as addressing likely uses of the instrument by teachers, administrators, and program evaluators.

JODY S. BRITTEN is Assistant Professor, Department of Educational Studies, Ball State University, Muncie, IN 47306 (E-mail: jsbritten@bsu.edu).
JERREL C. CASSADY is Associate Professor, Department of Educational Psychology, Ball State University, Muncie, IN 47306 (E-mail: jccassady@bsu.edu).

[Haworth co-indexing entry note]: "The Technology Integration Assessment Instrument: Understanding Planned Use of Technology by Classroom Teachers." Britten, Jody S., and Jerrel C. Cassady. Co-published simultaneously in *Computers in the Schools* (The Haworth Press, Inc.) Vol. 22, No. 3/4, 2005, pp. 49-61; and: *Classroom Integration of Type II Uses of Technology in Education* (ed: Cleborne D. Maddux, and D. LaMont Johnson) The Haworth Press, Inc., 2005, pp. 49-61. Single or multiple copies of this article are available for a fee from The Haworth Document Delivery Service [1-800-HAWORTH, 9:00 a.m. - 5:00 p.m. (EST). E-mail address: docdelivery@haworthpress.com].

Available online at http://www.haworthpress.com/web/CITS

doi:10.1300/J025v22n03_05

KEYWORDS. Assessment, evaluation, planning, integration, lesson plans, process-oriented, product-oriented, Technology Integration Assessment Instrument

UNDERSTANDING TECHNOLOGY USE IN INSTRUCTIONAL PLANNING OF CLASSROOM TEACHERS

Although technology in the classroom is typically deemed to be a positive shift in the betterment of students' post-school skills, simply placing technology in the classroom is not enough (Burke, 2000). As argued by Cuban (2001), access to technology does not translate into the use of that technology by classroom teachers. Therefore, to effectively measure technology integration, evaluators need to focus on how the technology is implemented in the classroom, not merely document available materials (Dockstader, 1999). Another problem in assessing technology integration has been the common problem of poor operational definitions for "technology" (Moersch, 1995). With respect to this paper we identify technology as computers, regardless of standard contextual setting (i.e., lab versus classroom use).

The International Society for Technology in Education (ISTE) technology standards provide a foundation for goal setting and the longitudinal tracking of technology use by classroom teachers. Central to the technology standards for teachers (NETS-T) is attention to the use of technology for the purpose of improving instructional design and outcomes (NETS Project, 2003). The presence of these standards in P-12 settings is just now becoming an embedded part of school-reform efforts. However, as the implementation of these standards is in its infancy, one of the lessons learned with regard to implementing curriculum standards in the P-12 setting is that standards must be aligned with professional evaluation, and natural responsibilities of classroom teachers (Turnbaugh Lockwood, 1999). Thus, we assert that it is critical to the successful infusion of technology standards that there be a means by which classroom teachers can identify the connections among standards, best practices in teaching, and uses of technology.

Effective use of technology to support learning is distinctly related to classroom teachers' understandings for different modes of technology use, basic understanding of technology, beliefs about instruction, and ability to motivate students to use the technology (Maddux & Cummings, 1986; MacArthur, 2001). However, determining efficacy is difficult because it is often unclear in what ways teachers' use of technology supports instructional goals (see Cuban, 2001). Thus, attempts to classify instructional uses for technology need to be framed within the standard language and context of P-12 educational settings.

As defined by Maddux (1986), classification of technology use can be summarized into two critical types. Type I applications of technology are defined as being passive or teacher-centered. Maddux defined Type II applications of technology as more learner-centered, and those that hold the potential to alter the effectiveness of teaching and ultimately the success of learning. While this dichotomy provides a basic framework, we argue that there is a need for an instrument by which teachers can assess their use and make data-driven decisions specific to their application of technology in the classroom.

ASSESSING THE ARTICULATION OF TECHNOLOGY INTEGRATION IN LESSON PLANS

The need in the field for lesson plan rating systems specific to technology integration is expected to increase in upcoming years (Brooks-Young, 2002). Administratively, such a rating system can provide a point of dialogue during evaluation conferences specific to technology application by classroom teachers (Brooks-Young, 2002; Darling-Hammond, Wise, & Pease, 1983). Given that technology is of growing importance to schools and that sizable portions of operating budgets are focused on technology purchases, it is imperative that administrators establish a better understanding of how teachers are using technology to support instruction and enhance student learning (Department of Education, 1999). However, many school administrators are in need of sound evaluative tools to make this internal assessment process reliable.

Another reason for the need for a systematic scoring rubric for lesson plans is based on the need in program evaluation to establish program success through triangulation. To effectively measure success of many educational technology initiatives, it is required that the evaluators demonstrate change in teacher behaviors. This has traditionally been accomplished through classroom observation, survey data, loose estimations of teacher lesson plans, or more holistic organizational analyses (Bober, 2002; Yepes-Baraya, 2002). Although several strategies have been employed to examine the level of integration of technology in the classroom, no measure examining teachers' use of technology through archived lesson plans that are aligned with NETS-T has been established.

Through our own work with evaluating technology innovation projects, we have seen the wealth of extant data available in the form of lesson plans. Using existing lesson plans that have been constructed within a framework of progressive change toward improved use of technology in education has several advantages. First, there is little logistical strain to the evaluation. School administrators or program evaluators can examine progress of several teachers in one "session," without having to schedule school-hour observation time. Second, the lesson plans maintain a higher degree of validity in response than self-report instruments. Third, the use of lesson plans as an evaluative data set provides a greater level of contextual validity in the analyses. Attention to the contextual factors in the given educational environment is a necessity for meaningful use of the TIAI as well as for the generalization of results.

The Technology Integration Assessment Instrument was designed to enable teachers, administrators, and evaluators to systematically examine the level and style of technology integration in a standard classroom application.

USING THE TECHNOLOGY INTEGRATION ASSESSMENT INSTRUMENT

The Technology Integration Assessment Instrument (TIAI), as seen in the Appendix, provides for ratings across seven dimensions of a lesson plan, with four levels of classification within each dimension. The classifications represent a continuum of technology integration; the labels are (a) Technology Not Present, (b) Non-Essential Technology Component, (c) Supportive Technology Component, and (d) Essential Technology Component. A brief description of each dimension follows, with a small set of examples to illustrate the types of activities within each level of classification. Note that the rubric itself (Appendix) encompasses these definitions; however, the descriptions to follow do not repeat that content.

We created the TIAI in an attempt to evaluate the progress teachers made over the course of one project that used the school classroom as a central point of intervention for overcoming the digital divide in a diverse community. An initial attempt at classifying lesson plans made use of a simple holistic rating driven by the school district's existing guidelines. That original rating system proved to be unreliable due to the holistic approach to rating. Subsequent to configuring the TIAI to provide specific evaluative data on the seven specific dimensions, the ratings generated through evaluating teachers' lesson plans met a higher standard of psychometric qualifications. In a random selection of teachers' lesson plans extending across all academic disciplines, inter-rater reliability estimates exceeded .70 across each dimension. In addition to demonstrating a high degree of 1:1 correspondence in ratings provided by the two independently trained raters, our examination of the ratings revealed that, in those cases where the ratings did not agree, the two responses were typically adjacent to each other on the rubric. As a second test of the utility of the TIAI, we compared teachers' selected lesson plans from within the same semester of instruction, also generating a high level of concordance in the dimension-specific technology integration estimations. In addition to these estimations of consistency in response across raters and across lessons, the trained raters were interviewed regarding the usability of the TIAI. One rater was a graduate student in education with experience in teaching and developing lesson plans. The second rater was a graduate student in school psychology with expertise in standardized testing and assessment. Both found the rubric easy to learn and free from ambiguity.

Planning

The planning dimension focused on the teachers' use of technology to locate, evaluate, select, and organize lesson activities. That is, the lesson itself does not depend upon the technology, and it would be possible to create or locate lesson-planning processes in the absence of the technology tools (Type I application). Technology is supportive in conditions when it is clear that not only was the computer used for planning, but that the lesson plan itself identified technology tools (i.e., hardware and/or software) that would be necessary to implement the lesson. Such a lesson that makes use of technology as a supportive component may be one that mentions using a pre-packaged PowerPoint presentation for the day's lecture. Although the technology provides support to the learning situation, it is not essential to meet the learning objectives, because the PowerPoint slides could merely be run off on a transparency, or the instructor could work without the visual aids (Type I application). Finally, those lessons that offer technology as an essential component demonstrate the development of a lesson that cannot be prepared without using technology tools (Type II application). Thus, these lessons often result in using technology as either a content-delivery mechanism (e.g., use of an Integrated Learning System) or an essential resource that makes the learning event possible (e.g., data probes connected to a statistical package for biology laboratory experiments).

Standards Relation (Content and NETS-Students)

The attention to standards is a common focus in recent years given pressure from federal and state mandates to demonstrate and promote effective planning related to core objectives and goals. For content standards, the focus of the rubric is on the level of technology integration into the targeted standards for the lesson. That is, rather than merely identifying that the instructor has linked the lesson to content standards or demonstrated that technology is evident in the lesson, our tool examines the level to which the standards are addressed *as a consequence* of the presence of the technology tools or materials. The most common example of non-essential uses of technology are word-processing programs used to complete written work that does not involve a write-and-rewrite process (e.g., typing spelling word lists). Supportive technology may include using Web-based search engines, or word-processing tools (Type I application). Essential uses of technology may include lessons requiring using a technology program for analyzing data (provided the standard was targeting data analyses) or using a computer assisted drawing program (CAD) for completing a project (Type II application).

NETS for Students (NETS-S; NETS Project, 2000) are becoming more commonly addressed as school districts recognize the importance of lifelong learning and employability associated with technology skills. Essentially, this dimension examines the level to which teachers have explicitly identified and incorporated NETS-S into the activity or lesson itself, with attention to developmental appropriateness.

Student Needs

Essentially, most proponents of educational technology applications promote the notion that individualized learning experiences or differentiated learning is improved in technology-rich classrooms. Although this is a common promise of educational technology, it is clearly not a realized vision in many educational settings. Non-essential uses of technology in this dimension include having all students complete an online or CD-ROM tutorial that does not adjust for individual learners (Type I application). Supportive technology may involve delivering lesson plans that can be preset to provide content at varied degrees of difficulty, either established by the user or in advance by the teacher (Type II application). Such "difficulty level" adjustments are common in skills-development software or games, but should not be confused with individualized instruction attempts afforded with programs that fall into the category of Integrated Learning Systems. Finally, essential technology focuses on providing differentiated instructional opportunities to children that could not be accomplished without technology tools (Type II application). In this way, the technology should be viewed as a tool that may provide remediation as well as enrichment for students, as the need may exist. Such programs generally have a control process through which the teacher can determine the order or presentation of learning materials, or allow the user to self-select content that is appropriate to her/his interests and skill level.

Implementation: Learning and Teaching

The implementation dimensions focus on using technology for both teaching and learning, recognizing the unique differences between these two processes. Implementation for learning focuses on using technology in the classroom as a means to boost students' understanding of the content, or to engage students in the core activity through the assistance of technology (Type II application). The implementation of technology for teaching dimension examines the level to which the teacher relies upon the technology during an instructional session to deliver the content (Type I or Type II application). This dimension is intended to discriminate among the lessons that make use of technology at rudimentary levels (Type I application) and those that make the technology an integral part of the instructional process (Type II application).

A helpful distinction identified in the rubric itself focuses on technology that is used in a process-oriented versus product-oriented activity. Product orientations typically make use of the technology tool as a useful but not necessary feature (Type I application). There is a common experience in observing lessons where teachers use technology, but the implementation really provides no additional gains to the learning environment and generally could be considered a wasteful use of resources. For example, one application suggested in a reviewed lesson was to provide all students with wireless devices so they could follow the class lecture PowerPoint slides from their own desks. The students in this setting would have no additional access to material; the teacher planned to still display the PowerPoint slides on the front board to keep everyone on the same topic, and there was no intention to expand the level of interaction among students using the wireless units.

Using technology in a supportive fashion generally can be seen in situations where the teacher is able to call up additional resources in a quick manner, or deliver divergent content to students with differential needs with ease (Type II application). The essential distinction between this rating and the "essential" category rests on identifying of the possibility to deliver content in the absence of the specified technology (Type II application). If the learning goals of the lesson could still be met without the technology tools, then they are merely supportive to those tasks. Generally, this distinction is tied to the presence of attention to technology skills as a meaningful focus of at least part of the curriculum (i.e., NETS-S focus).

Implementing technology for student learning examines the lesson from the perspective of the student as technology user. From a learning perspective, we define non-essential technology as those technical tools or procedures that clearly provide opportunities for students to use technology, but the use of technology itself is not anticipated to support or promote learning. Examples include word processing for spelling words, e-mail access for "penpals," and using a digital paint program to design a cover for the student's self-authored book. Supportive technology tools promote the learning environment, but only through efficiency or access to additional resources that would not be possible otherwise. Examples of these include using word-processing programs in the editing process, accessing content experts through discussion boards, or viewing online photos of historical documents or materials. Finally, essential technology components provide an undeniable and irreplaceable learning benefit for students, by exposing the learner to content that is not available in any other format, or by providing the learner with a method of interacting that is enabled only through digital media.

Assessment

One often-overlooked area of lesson development when examining lesson plans is the connection to assessment. Once again, the varied levels of classification for this dimension are primarily influenced by the ability to assess the learner in the absence of technology. Non-essential uses of technology are characterized by lessons that make use of technology, but in which no assessment of the outcome product or developed skills related to the learning process is undertaken (Type I application). Supportive technology makes use of technology to deliver assessment or focuses on the product of a technology-driven activity in determining mastery (Type II application). Finally, essential technology builds upon the expectations for supportive technology by requiring that the assessment be impossible in the absence of technology, such as through a demonstrated procedural skill involving technology application (Type II). There is also the expectation that the lesson will include assessment of mastery of NETS-S (or an alternate technology standards system) by the learners.

USE OF RATINGS

Once the ratings in each dimension have been recorded, the process of categorizing the level of technology integration exhibited in the lesson begins. As mentioned earlier, it is not reasonable to generate holistic ratings in most cases due to the threats to validity and internal reliability inherent when condensing multiple distinct categories. For example, a teacher who clearly makes use of essential technologies in the classroom but fails to identify a method of assessment or list standards for the lesson would receive an overall rating that was equivalent to a teacher with primarily non-essential uses of technology but who had made mention of the content standards and assessment practices.

Consequently, the Technology Integration Assessment Instrument rating is best used as a measure of strengths and weaknesses across the seven dimensions of lesson planning. As alluded to earlier, we see two primary contributions this instrument can make to the process of integrating technology into educational environments. First, the rubric can be used as an evaluative measure for projects with a focus on teacher integration of educational technology. The lesson plan analyses afforded with this tool exceed most pre-existing measures, and allow for triangulation of data in typical educational technology evaluation plans. As an evaluation instrument, the rubric can track change over time, diagnose patterns of strengths and weaknesses, and allow for comparisons among control and experimental conditions.

The second anticipated use of this Technology Integration Assessment Instrument is within the P-12 school itself, either as a personal reflection or an action research tool. Teachers or administrators who are consciously attempting to increase the level of technology integration (i.e., from Type I to Type II) in the daily education of their students will benefit from periodic, or representative, use of this rubric. Teachers may find it useful as a before-and-after picture of their technology integration following technology-focused professional growth activities, or as a means of documenting proficiency in technology for performance-based reviews or application to tenure status. As a tool employed for action research, the teacher may simultaneously ask students about their interest or satisfaction in the specific lesson plans, and compare student responses based on the overall level of technology integration in the seven dimensions. Similarly, comparisons on student achievement could be tracked in relation to level of technology integration, identifying the level of impact of each dimension on these important outcome measures.

CONCLUSIONS

While we acknowledge that using an instrument to rate the level of technology integration in teacher-created lesson plans could be observed as somewhat controversial, it is important to note that in this era of accountability there must be efforts made to accomplish goals and mandates of accountability within the natural work of classroom teachers. In addition, while assessment specific to technology use by teachers has been explored (NETS Project, 2003), we have observed a trend where the assessment of technology use has been disassociated with the assessment of other critical instructional factors. This rubric is intended to provide teachers, administrators, or program evaluators with a consistent framework for articulating how technology is used and, more importantly, how that technology is integrally tied to critical pedagogical features such as assessment, individualized attention to student needs, and addressing educational standards.

In efforts to increase the Type II application of technology in the classroom, it is important to continue searching for a valid instrument to assess use, but it is also critical to have a data-driven decision-making context for providing technology-focused professional development. The only way to reasonably expect technology to positively impact the learning of P-12 students is through the expectation of teachers to meaningfully apply those technologies in an instructional setting (Cradler, 1992). We believe that the TIAI can help teachers and program implementers more effectively assess the development of these skills and practices in classroom settings. The TIAI is a flexible tool that enables the user to explore individual growth in select dimensions as well as provides the opportunity to examine an entire district perspective in overall technology integration across the seven dimensions.

REFERENCES

Bober, M. J. (2002). Teacher outcomes: Changed pedagogy. In J. Johnston & L. Toms Barker (Eds.), *Assessing the impact of technology in teaching and learning* (pp. 87-118). Ann Arbor, MI: Institute for Social Research.

Brooks-Young, S. (2002). *Making technology standards work for you–A guide for school administrators.* Washington, DC: International Society for Technology in Education.

Burke, J. (2000). *New directions: Teacher technology standards.* Atlanta, GA: Southern Regional Education Board.

Cradler, J. (1992). *Comprehensive study of educational technology programs in California authorized from 1984-1992.* San Francisco: Far West Laboratory for Educational Research and Development.

Cuban, L. (2001) Teachers' infrequent computer use in classrooms. In J. Woodward & L. Cuban (Eds.), *Technology, curriculum, and professional development* (pp. 121-137). Thousand Oaks, CA: Corwin Press.

Darling-Hammond, L., Wise, A., & Pease S. (1983). Teacher evaluation in the organizational context: A review of the literature. *Review of Educational Research, 53,* 285-237.

Dockstader, J. (1999). Teachers of the 21st century know the what, why, and how of technology integration. *T.H.E. Journal, 26*(6), 73-74.

MacArthur, C. (2001). Technology implementation in special education. In J. Woodward & L. Cuban (Eds.), *Technology, curriculum, and professional development* (pp. 115-120). Thousand Oaks, CA: Corwin Press.

Maddux, C. (1986). Microcomputers in education and counseling: Problems and cautions. *Techniques, 2*(1), 9-14.

Maddux, C., & Cummings, R. (1986). Educational computing at the crossroads: Type I or Type II uses to predominate? *Educational Technology, 26*(7), 34-38.

Moersch, C. (1995). Levels of technology implementation (LoTi): A framework for measuring classroom technology use. *Learning and Leading with Technology, 23*(3), 40-42.

NETS Project. (2000). *National educational technology standards for students–Connecting curriculum and technology.* Washington, DC: International Society for Technology in Education.

NETS Project. (2003). *National educational technology standards for teachers–Resources for assessment.* Washington, DC: International Society for Technology in Education.

Roblyer, M. (2003). Getting our NETS worth: The role of ISTE's National Educational Technology Standards. *Learning and Leading with Technology, 30*(8), 6-13.

Turnbaugh Lockwood, A. (1999). *Standards: From policy to practice.* Thousand Oaks, CA: Corwin Press.

U.S. Department of Education. (1999). *Preparing tomorrow's teachers to use technology.* Washington, DC: Author. Retrieved October 15, 2003, from http://www.ed.gov/teachtech/.

Yepes-Baraya, M. (2002). Technology integration. In J. Johnston & L. Toms Barker (Eds.), *Assessing the impact of technology in teaching and learning* (pp. 139-160). Ann Arbor, MI: Institute for Social Research.

APPENDIX

Technology Integration Assessment Instrument

Dimension	Technology not present	Non-essential technology component	Supportive technology component	Essential technology component
Planning (materials, equipment, etc.)	No mention of technology.	Uses technology in lesson not related to the addressed standards.	Uses computer to plan for lesson. Makes mention of necessary equipment and technologies for replication purposes.	Computer is essential to planning of lesson (e.g., WebQuest). Equipment and technologies are built into lesson design and objectives, and are discussed within the context of the lesson and not as an external component.
Standards (content standards per grade level and content area)	No mention of technology. OR No mention of content standards.	Uses computer to plan for lesson.	Uses technology supports or promotes the acquisition of standards in the lesson, but is not directly tied to the standard itself.	Technology use in the lesson is directly linked to one or more standards, making acquisition of that standard possible.
Standards (NETS-S)	No mention of technology. OR No mention of NETS.	NETS are present but not identified or embedded into lesson as a learning goal. NETS addressed are not up to expected grade level.	NETS are present but not identified or embedded into lesson as a learning goal. NETS are grade-level appropriate.	NETS are present and integrated into grade-level appropriate learning goals.
Attention to student needs	No mention of technology.	Technology is not used in an adaptable fashion. All students use same technology tool or complete same technology-based activity.	Technology can be modified by the teacher or student to meet the needs of students from diverse backgrounds.	Technology is the only means by which this lesson can be adapted to meet the needs of students from diverse backgrounds; that is, the technology tool or activity is designed to be adaptive.

Implementation (use of technology in learning)	No mention of technology.	Technology is not expected to directly impact learning.	Learning is impacted in time, quality, or wealth of resources by the use of technology.	Technology impacts learning by presentation, product, or process.
Implementation (use of technology in teaching)	No mention of technology.	Lesson uses technology but does not impact implementation (product-oriented technology).	Lesson is facilitated with technology, but learning goals could be achieved without technology in place (process-oriented and/or product-oriented technology).	Equipment and technologies are built into lesson design and objectives and are discussed within the context of the lesson and not as an external component. Lesson requires the use of technology (process and product are dependent upon technology).
Assessment	No mention of assessment. OR No mention of technology.	Technology is not used in the assessment component (neither the use of technology nor a product of technology).	Technology-based product is assessed, or technology application is used to deliver and/or score the assessment instrument. However, similar assessment could be replicated without technology.	Technology products and/or processes are directly assessed, or assessment relies upon the use of technology for delivery or collection. Identified assessment could not be conducted without technology. NETS are identified as part of assessment.

Karen Dutt-Doner
Susan M. Allen
Daniel Corcoran

Transforming Student Learning by Preparing the Next Generation of Teachers for Type II Technology Integration

SUMMARY. Integrating Type II technology applications into the school is problematic. One method of facilitating this is through pre-service teacher preparation. Pre-service teachers have "grown up digital," but being comfortable with technology is not adequate preparation for understanding how to meaningfully integrate technology. This is because meaningful technology integration is not so much a technological endeavor as it is a pedagogical one. This case study from a pre-service graduate teacher education program at a private university illustrates how technical literacy, Web resources, meaningful technology teaching experiences, and a culture of collaboration were

KAREN DUTT-DONER is Associate Professor, Niagara University, Department of Education, Niagara University, NY 14109 (E-mail: kdd@niagara.edu).
SUSAN M. ALLEN is Director of Libraries and Academic Technologies, Nichols School, Williamsville, NY 14221 (E-mail: sallen@nicholsschool.org).
DANIEL CORCORAN is Educational Consultant at Nichols School, Williamsville, NY 14221 (E-mail: corcorand626@yahoo.com).

[Haworth co-indexing entry note]: "Transforming Student Learning by Preparing the Next Generation of Teachers for Type II Technology Integration." Dutt-Doner, Karen, Susan M. Allen, and Daniel Corcoran. Co-published simultaneously in *Computers in the Schools* (The Haworth Press, Inc.) Vol. 22, No. 3/4, 2005, pp. 63-75; and: *Classroom Integration of Type II Uses of Technology in Education* (ed: Cleborne D. Maddux, and D. LaMont Johnson) The Haworth Press, Inc., 2005, pp. 63-75. Single or multiple copies of this article are available for a fee from The Haworth Document Delivery Service [1-800-HAWORTH, 9:00 a.m. - 5:00 p.m. (EST). E-mail address: docdelivery@haworthpress.com].

Available online at http://www.haworthpress.com/web/CITS

doi:10.1300/J025v22n03_06

integrated into the curriculum. Its goal is to prepare the next generation of teachers to work with technology and library professionals to bring meaningful technology integration to students.

KEYWORDS. Pre-service teacher education, technology integration, elementary education, digitized primary source documents, information literacy, library media specialist

How do we actually get Type II applications into the school to facilitate student learning? That is, how do we effect change in the school, to foster the use of technology not just to automate the same old exercises, but to actively engage the learner?

We could approach the problem from several angles, including curriculum development, leadership initiatives, or professional development of teachers. But, research has shown that imposing change on experienced teachers can be a challenge (Hargreaves & Fullan, 1992) and is often unsuccessful (Hargreaves & Dawe, 1989; Huberman & Miles, 1984). One unique opportunity for facilitating change as called for by National Educational Technology Standards (NETS) (ISTE, 2002) and *Learning for the 21st* Century (Partnership for 21st Century Skills, 2003) is pre-service teacher preparation.

The new NETS for teachers (ISTE, 2002) call on teacher educators to prepare prospective teachers to empower students learning through the use of Type II technology applications: those applications that enhance the process of learning, not just teaching. And the NETS call on practicing teachers to transform their pedagogy to incorporate technology-enriched strategies aimed at the same purpose (ISTE, 2002, p. 5).

We now know that simply supplying schools with computers and providing skills-based training does not effectively prepare teachers for the complexity of transforming their practice (Collins, 1996; Means, 1994). In addition, research indicates that many teacher candidates are not successfully prepared to carry out the necessary task of technology-enriched classroom practice (Moursound & Bielfeldt, 1999; Willis & Mehlinger, 1996). Moursound and Bielfieldt (1999) encourage teacher-training institutions to add to technology proficiency of new teachers through integrated coursework, to engage in technology planning that focuses not only on facilities but on the integration of IT in teaching and learning, to provide student teachers with supervised opportunities to integrate technology during field experiences, and to encourage faculty to model and integrate technology (p. 3).

Today's pre-service candidates are a good case in point: They have "grown up digital," and as such are ready for and, most importantly, open to technology integration. But in working with teacher candidates, we have learned that growing up digital is not adequate preparation for understanding how to meaningfully integrate technology to transform learning. This has led us to the conclusion that development, execution, and assessment of successful Type II technology applications must be taught, modeled, exercised, and assessed as embedded curriculum within the teacher preparation program.

What follows is a case study from a pre-service graduate teacher education program at a private university. This case study illustrates how we incorporated technical literacy, Web resources, meaningful technology teaching experiences, and a culture of collaboration into the curriculum, with the goal of preparing the next generation of teachers to work with technology and library professionals to bring meaningful technology integration to their students.

CASE STUDY

In the one-year graduate program leading to a master's degree in education, teacher candidates complete certification requirements to teach in a state and/or the province of a foreign country. The core education curriculum is comprised of nine courses, including multicultural education; human development; special needs; foundations of education; reading methods; language arts methods; general methods; methods of math, science, and social studies; student teaching; and a student-teaching seminar. The program incorporates topics such as preparation for the integration of technology into the curriculum, research skills, development of information literacy instruction, and the integration of arts into the curriculum.

This case study focuses on Type II technology integration that takes place in an interdisciplinary math, science, and social studies methods course. Teacher candidates come from a variety of backgrounds: urban/rural, recent grads/older students, and almost equally from two countries. Consequently, there is a great diversity of experience, both with technology and with education standards. Most have fairly good technology skills, but are not as proficient in the broader area of information literacy (e.g., knowing where on the Web to look for resources or how to read a Web address).

Most apparent was that teacher candidates were not adequately prepared to integrate technology into their students' lessons in a meaningful way, even those who were the most tech-savvy. And with good reason: Meaningful technology integration is not so much a technical endeavor as a pedagogical one.

Objectives

Throughout this course, there is a clear connection between curriculum development, student learning standards, meeting diverse student needs, constructivist practices, and the role that technology plays in enhancing student learning. This course provides an arena for embedding Type II technologies, with the goal of arming teacher candidates with a collection of technology-enriched teaching strategies in math, science, and social studies (*Niagara University Graduate Catalog*, 2003, p. 40). The International Society for Technology in Education (2002) calls for the technology integration focus on helping pre-service teacher candidates "plan and design effective learning environments and experiences supported by technology" (p. 14) and "implement curriculum plans that include methods and strategies for applying technology to maximize student learning" (p. 14).

Methodology

Three areas of technology integration were the focus for this case study: practicing *collaboration* as a strategy for technology integration (ISTE, 2002; Means & Olson, 1997), using *digitized primary source documents* as a means of active problem solving to construct knowledge about a historical event and/or time period (Wineburg, 1991), and *leveraging technology* to encourage active learning in the classroom (Boethel & Dimock, 1999; Maddux, Johnson, & Willis, 2001).

Collaboration

Just as technology integration needs to be taught, modeled, and exercised, even to those with good technology skills, so does information literacy and the collaboration required to support it. Preparing today's teachers for the complex nature of classroom practice requires more integrated pedagogy, both in coursework and fieldwork. Teachers no longer work in isolation, but need the support and guidance of many other educational professionals, including the school library media specialist. They need to have the knowledge and experiences in order to function in this collaborative capacity.

In our collaborative work with teacher candidates, it became apparent that they had limited training in using technology to transform their practice, limited exposure in information literacy skills for themselves or their students, and no knowledge about working with the school library media specialist. As the research indicates, these are major oversights in the preparation of teachers (Moursound & Beilfeldt, 1999; Willis & Mehlinger, 1996).

In an effort to help teacher candidates better understand the collaborative nature of teaching and the necessity of using a variety of resources, collaborative education was modeled in an experiential-based curriculum with the aim of increasing teacher candidates' library and information technology skills in order to transform pedagogy. Specifically, the role of the school library media specialist was introduced into their preparation, working with them on technology integration and information literacy skills. Throughout this introduction we discuss, model, and assign collaborative work with a library media specialist. The goal is to provide expectations and experiences of successful collaboration even before the teacher candidate enters the school, so that this will become an integral part of his/her everyday practice. This collaborative model provides the foundation on which information literacy skills and technology-enriched practices are built.

DIGITIZED PRIMARY SOURCE DOCUMENTS

Using digitized primary source documents is an obvious area for the next generation of teachers to concentrate, as strategists recommend instruction in visual literacy and critical-thinking skills, and standardized tests require proficiency in document-based queries and constructed-response queries. Before teacher candidates can proficiently use technology to examine primary sources, they need to understand what a primary source is and why it is important.

Learning About Primary Source Teaching

The "Mind-Walk" exercise found on the Library of Congress American Memory Web site (http://memory.loc.gov) is used so students can understand the nature of artifacts and how they can be interpreted. The exercise starts by asking teacher candidates to record how many primary sources they create in a single day, and to appreciate the volume of documents that technology makes available to them. Technology has revolutionized access to primary source documents: Until very recently only a few were available to a few, but now millions are available to those with the technology and the knowledge to use them. Thus, students are provided with new opportunities to work like historians in interpreting and analyzing historical truth, no longer relying on others' interpretations of history from textbooks. This is an excellent example of Type II technology application.

Learning How Technology Enhances Primary Source Analysis

Before teacher candidates can use technology for primary source teaching, they need to understand what it takes for their students to get real value from primary source analysis. The impact technology has is discovered in a class exercise by looking at a photograph on the Library of Congress Web site that allows the reader to look close up at a photograph to see great detail (http://memory.loc.gov/ammem/ ndlpedu/educators/workshop/primary/examprim.html). Teacher candidates also examine how technology enhances their ability to research information about the primary sources online to have a better understanding of the historical context of the documents (http://memory.loc.gov/ammem/ndlpedu/lessons/98/labor/plan.html#procedure). Teacher candidates look at parts of a photograph in isolation, a technique available through technology, and discuss how it impacts interpretation, causing the reader to have deeper historical understanding and a stronger historical context to guide him/her (http://memory. loc.gov/ammem/ndlpedu/lessons/97/civilwar/civilwar.html).

Documents are introduced in both paper and online forms, which illustrates the differences in clarity and readability, and the context from which our excerpts were drawn. Teacher candidates evaluate the documents, using guidelines suggested by the Library of Congress (2004): *Scan* each document to see what you can learn from the document as a whole. *Examine* each document in detail to see what you can learn from the specifics. *Analyze* each document to draw your own conclusions. *Compare* the documents to each other to crosscheck your conclusions.

Small groups then debrief with the whole class to deconstruct their experience–not on the *results* of the analysis, but on the *process* using the following prompting questions: What *skills* are required for this analysis? What possible *stumbling blocks* might students encounter? How did you utilize your *background knowledge* in analyzing the documents? How did you or could you use *technology* to support further understanding about the primary source documents? How was learning about history using primary sources *different from other ways* that you have learned?

Among the possible problems discussed are: *vocabulary*–not only unfamiliar words, but also familiar ones whose outdated usage might be misinterpreted. For example, the picture of a tent city set up to house 1906 earthquake victims that is labeled "refugee camp"–a term which might have modern connotations that are misleading in this case. Also, *readability*–whether because old documents are physically illegible or because the reading level of the text is not appropriate to the grade level of the students. A technological tool called "Magic Lens" is demonstrated, which allows students to transcribe a select group of primary sources that may be difficult to read (http://memorialhall.mass.edu/activities/magic_lens/index.html). Teacher candidates then compare this exercise to an assignment that seeks to impart the same information from a traditional textbook. It is invariably apparent that when working with the primary documents, every group is actively engaged, animated, and collaborating.

Integrating Digitized Primary Sources into Classroom Practice

The second exercise requires students to locate and use available resources to incorporate primary sources in their lessons. One of the goals is to ensure that teacher candidates understand that they will not have time to create all lesson plans they need every day from scratch. Therefore, they need to learn to locate quality sources and adapt them for their own needs using online research resources, to work with experts like the library media specialist in their school, and to judge online resources for credibility.

Students work in teams of two, searching the online collections of the Library of Congress to find a lesson plan or other resource that they would like to use in their own classroom, and then adapt it as necessary to fit their needs. Adaptations are almost always required, either because the lessons tend to have been created with older students in mind, or because the technology anticipated to complete the exercise is not available. Sometimes, teachers have to make their own technology adaptations; other times, the creators of the exercise have made the necessary accommodations.

Learning is enhanced if the students have direct online access to the primary sources that allow for more thorough viewing, and to the research tools that can guide their analysis. But regardless of the level of technology that the teacher is able to incorporate, there is clear evidence of Type II technology integration, simply because the student learning is transformed by having access to digitized primary source documents. Students are actively engaged in critical analysis, piecing together information, interpretations, and perspectives. In some cases, differing perspectives of the same historical event unfold and need to be addressed through scaffolding (http://memory.loc.gov/ammem/ndlpedu/educators/workshop/primary/bloom.html). For many teacher candidates this method of learning is very different from their own elementary experience.

The teacher's role in this type of technology integration is also transformed, coaching students through their own exploration, rather than feeding students information. This role is modeled by suggesting sources and possible adaptations, as the teacher candidates complete their lesson development. For many teacher candidates, this role differs from their own personal experiences in which the teacher was the "giver" of information, rather than the guide toward learning. Modeling of the teacher's role becomes a critical component so that teacher candidates can have a better understanding of "what it looks like" to be a teacher in a Type II classroom.

Teacher candidates work in teams of two to complete a 30-minute lesson that incorporates digitized primary source documents, and then to teach it to another team of two during the class's next meeting. Teacher candidates share feedback, both positive and critical, so that the peer teaching is focused on learning to better understand this new methodology. Finally, teacher candidates individually reflect on their Type II technology planning and teaching experience to better understand what they learned, how this experience will impact their future teaching, and when and how the use of this technology-enriched teaching strategy is appropriate.

In their reflections, teacher candidates make connections between the role of technology and active student learning. They understand that using the Library of Congress allows them to teach in ways that are different from ways in which they were taught. Teacher candidates experience how primary sources actively engage students in constructing knowledge by providing relevant historical research, respecting and incorporating students' background knowledge, valuing their points of view, and adapting curriculum to address students' suppositions (Brooks & Brooks, 1999). As a result of this teaching and learning experience, teacher candidates have a better understanding of how a technological resource can support practice–practice that allows students to transform their knowledge through the creation of new understandings (Brooks & Brooks, 1999; Gardner, 1999). Research (Boethel & Dimock, 1999; Means & Olson, 1997) indicates that technology is most effective when used as tool to support a learning environment rather than the object of instruction.

In this way, technology integrated appropriately not only supports cognitive development but also supports affective development. Motivating students to intrinsically want to learn is just as important as the learning that takes place in the elementary classroom. It is apparent that the teacher's role is reconfigured when Type II technology is integrated and that teacher candidates benefit from opportunities to experience this new-found role.

USING TECHNOLOGY TO ENCOURAGE ACTIVE LEARNING

To better help teacher candidates understand how technology can be integrated across the curriculum, they examine and review various types of resources that are useful in Type II technology integration. The goal is to help them understand how technology application can actively engage learners, and begin to consider how to integrate technology into their lesson plans. This integration strategy will be required as part of the lesson plans developed and used in their assistantship field placements.

Type I versus Type II Technology Integration

We begin by reviewing the difference between Type I and Type II technology applications (Maddux, Johnson, & Willis, 2001) so that teacher candidates can consider the interconnectedness of technology and pedagogy. Research indicates that given the right conditions, technology can "accelerate, enrich and deepen basic skills, motivate and engage students in learning–and strengthen teaching" (Muir, 2001, p.1), a goal teacher candidates should achieve. In addition, the benefits that technology integration can bring to students by actively engaging them in learning are discussed. These discussions include topics such as: meeting the diverse learning styles of today's learners, motivating students with authentic learning experiences, increasing students' time on task, and sustaining positive attitudes in learning. Complete and lasting understanding requires that students become actively engaged in learning. The highest level of understanding and retention comes from the activities inherent in Type II technology integration. Once teacher candidates have a better understanding of why Type II technology integration is critical for supporting student learning, the goal is to help them build their repertoire of skills, knowledge, and experiences in ways to use technology to enhance student learning.

Teacher candidates need to understand the complexity of teaching in a technology-enriched environment, because students bring different background knowledge and different technology skills to the classroom. They need to make sure that the resources they develop or choose are age-appropriate, in both the substance they convey and the technology skills required to use them. The NETS standards (ISTE, 2002) are used as a gauge of age-appropriate technology, but also caution that students' actual skills may not meet these high standards.

Suggested Type II Technology Integration

The teacher assesses student learning as it is taking place and provides the necessary support through questioning, probing, guidance, and mini-teaching units, and emphasizes its importance in facilitating meaningful use of technology for educational ends. Video and digital cameras are discussed as ways of assessing student learning, graphic organizer software is presented to enhance students' ability to organize and represent connections between concepts, and multimedia presentation software is used to demonstrate ways to actively engage learners in a typically teacher-centered approach to instruction.

Web materials for teachers are explored that help them create their own resources for active learning. For example, *Filamentality* (http://www.kn.pacbell.com/wired/fil/guides.html) is a valuable resource, especially for neophytes to follow a few well-guided steps to create high-quality, well-targeted Web resources for students. Teachers can choose from several different page types, which helps to focus their learning objectives. Teachers who have already used *Filamentality* to create student learning resources can share them on the *Blue Web'n* site (http://www.kn.pacbell.com/wired/bluewebn/). While there is no quality control imposed on the materials posted here, they are well organized so teachers can easily browse them to find ready-to-use resources that fit their needs.

Teacher candidates explore various Type II technology applications focused on actively engaging learners while providing access to learning opportunities not available without technology. Their introduction to WebQuests starts with a "WebQuest about WebQuests" (http://www.geocities.com/techlabloms/Quest.htm), which helps them have a better understanding of the purpose and uses. This continues with exploration of The WebQuest Page (http://webquest.sdsu.edu/), a guide to templates for WebQuest development and links to teacher-developed WebQuests organized by subject and evaluated for quality. WebQuests provide opportunities for elementary students to use Web-based research tools to learn new information while becoming actively engaged in the learning process. This engaging learning experience provides long-lasting knowledge and culminates in the creation of a product that provides the teacher with authentic assessment data that learning took place.

Teacher candidates then explore virtual field trips–interactive tours of locations too remote to visit–so that their students can experience places they would never have an opportunity to see. One of the sites reviewed is *Museums Across the Curriculum* (http://www.techlearning.com/db_area/archives/TL/200103/museum7.html). We caution our students not to assume that all virtual field trips are Type II applications of technology and draw attention to the difference between *Castles on the Web* (http://www.castlesontheweb.com/search/Castle_Tours/) and *Design Your Own Robot* (http://www.mos.org/exhibits/robot/). It is apparent that in some cases, these virtual field trips are simply photographs placed online. While this may still provide a valuable resource for students, it does not offer an interactive feature that contributes to the learning that can take place as a result of visiting–a necessity for a Type II technology.

We explore *simulation* resources that would be impossible without technology, including *The Underground Railroad* (http://www.nationalgeographic.com/railroad/), *Xpeditions* (http://www.nationalgeographic.com/xpeditions/hall/index.html), *Animated Atlas* (http://www.animatedatlas.com/), and *Virtual Math Manipulatives* (http://matti.usu.edu/nlvm/nav/index.html). These simulations are intended to provide opportunities to recreate experiences that would not be available otherwise. But, these sites also require students to actively engage in critical thinking by making decisions–a process that deepens the learning that takes place.

Finally, we discuss the development and use of *treasure hunts* such as *Collection of Treasure Hunts* (http://www.ctnba.org/ctn/k8/treasure.html) and *Black History* (http://www.kn.pacbell.com/wired/BHM/hunt.html) that help students learn to search the Web while practicing problem-solving skills.

Integrating Type II Technologies into Teacher Candidates' Practice

Once teacher candidates are introduced to these new resources, they work in groups for structured exploration to better understand how to integrate the technology into practice. Using the NETS for Teachers and Students (ISTE, 2002), teacher candidates identify one technology they can integrate into their teaching and present it to the rest of the class. In their presentation, they demonstrate the technology, and discuss how it would be used in an age-appropriate classroom, and its connection to the NETS for Students and Teachers (ISTE, 2002).

Some of these resources are further integrated into the course as the instructor models them, followed by deconstructing of the teaching/learning experience from a student's and teacher's perspective. This debriefing provides teacher candidates the opportunity to better understand the complex decision-making process that is taking place before, during, and after instruction. Teacher candidates indicate that they learn best from these modeling and debriefing experiences because they provide a critical context for helping them make pedagogical decisions.

Having explored these technologies, they are then required to integrate them into lesson plans subsequently taught in elementary classrooms, linking their pedagogy to the NETS for Teachers and Students (ISTE, 2002). This has two purposes. First, teacher candidates experience technology-integrated teaching in a supportive environment with an expert teacher who provides feedback. Second, teacher candidates model effective examples of Type II technology integration for more experienced teachers who may not be aware of the technology application.

FINAL THOUGHTS

In this model, we come full circle in the professional development of both pre-service and in-service teachers, transforming educational practice in an effort to enhance the learning experiences of students in our classrooms through technology.

REFERENCES

Boethel, M., & Dimock, K. V. (1999). *Constructing knowledge with technology: A review of the literature*. Southwest Educational Development Laboratories. Retrieved February 26, 2004, from SEDL database: http://www.sedl.org/pubs/tec27/flash.html

Brooks, J. G., & Brooks, M. G. (1999). *In search of understanding. The case of the constructivist classrooms*. Alexandria, VA: Association for Supervision and Curriculum Development.

Collins, B. (1996). The Internet as an educational innovation: Lessons from experience with computer implementation. *Educational Technology, 36*(6), 21-30.

Gardner, H. (1999). *Intelligence reframed: Multiple intelligences for the 21st century*. New York: Basic Books.

Hargreaves, A., & Dawe, R. (1989). *Coaching as unreflective practice: Contrived collegiality or collaborative culture*. Paper presented at American Educational Research Association, Chicago, IL.

Hargreaves, A., & Fullan, M. (1992). *Understanding teacher development*. New York: Teachers College Press.

Huberman, M., & Miles, M. (1984). *Innovation up close*. New York: Plenum.

International Society for Technology in Education. (2002). *National educational technology standards for teachers: Preparing teachers to use technology*. Danvers, MA: Author.

Library of Congress. (2004). *Evaluating primary sources*. Retrieved February 26, 2004, from http://memory.loc.gov/ammem/ndlpedu/educators/workshop/primary/whatsee.html.

Maddux, C. D., Johnson, D. L., & Willis, J. W. (2001). *Educational computing: Learning with tomorrows technologies* (3rd ed.). Boston: Allyn & Bacon.

Means, B. (1994). Using technology to advance educational goals. In *Technology and education reform* (pp. 1-22). San Francisco: Jossey-Bass.

Means, B., & Olson, K. (1997). *Technology and education reform*. Washington, DC: U.S. Department of Education.

Moursound, D., & Bielfeldt, T. (1999). *Will new teachers be prepared to teach in the digital age?* Retrieved February 26, 2004, from the Milken Exchange on Education Technology: http://www.mff.org/publications/publications.taf?page=154.

Muir, M. (2001). *Overview of integrating technology into the curriculum*. Retrieved February 26, 2004, from Maine Center for Meaningful Engaged Learning Web site: http://www.mcmel.org/tech/overview.html.

Niagara University Graduate Catalog. (2003). Niagara Falls, NY: Niagara University.

Partnership for 21st Century Skills. (2003). *Learning for the 21st century*. Washington, DC: Author.

Willis, J. W. & Mehlinger, H. (1996). Information technology and teacher education. In J. P. Sikula (Ed.), *Handbook on research in teacher education* (pp. 978-1029). New York: Macmillan.

Wineburg, S. S. (1991). Historical problem solving: A study of the cognitive processes used in the evaluation of documentary and pictorial evidence. *Journal of Educational Psychology, 83*(1), 73-87.

Kathleen M. Gabric
Christina Z. Hovance
Sharon L. Comstock
Delwyn L. Harnisch

Scientists in Their Own Classroom: The Use of Type II Technology in the Science Classroom

SUMMARY. This paper represents and contextualizes the use of advanced technologies in a high school biology classroom to enhance inquiry in traditional science curriculum by drawing upon two years' worth of data. This paper presents the research-practitioners' reflections and understanding of the application of Type II technology's impact when integrated in service to authentic science education at the secondary level. The goal of this paper is twofold: (a) to demonstrate the effectiveness of Type II applications of technology in creating an environment that allows students to be scientists in their own classroom, and

KATHLEEN M. GABRIC is High School Teacher, Hinsdale Central High School, Hinsdale, IL 60521 (E-mail: kgabric@Hinsdale86.org).
CHRISTINA Z. HOVANCE is High School Teacher, Hinsdale Central High School, Hinsdale, IL 60521 (E-mail: chovance@Hinsdale86.org).
SHARON L. COMSTOCK is a doctoral student, University of Illinois at Urbana-Champaign, Champaign, IL 60527 (E-mail: slcomstock@sbcglobal.net).
DELWYN L. HARNISCH is Professor, University of Nebraska, Lincoln, NE 68588 (E-mail: harnisch@unl.edu).

[Haworth co-indexing entry note]: "Scientists in Their Own Classroom: The Use of Type II Technology in the Science Classroom." Gabric et al. Co-published simultaneously in *Computers in the Schools* (The Haworth Press, Inc.) Vol. 22, No. 3/4, 2005, pp. 77-91; and: *Classroom Integration of Type II Uses of Technology in Education* (ed: Cleborne D. Maddux, and D. LaMont Johnson) The Haworth Press, Inc., 2005, pp. 77-91. Single or multiple copies of this article are available for a fee from The Haworth Document Delivery Service [1-800-HAWORTH, 9:00 a.m. - 5:00 p.m. (EST). E-mail address: docdelivery@haworthpress.com].

Available online at http://www.haworthpress.com/web/CITS

doi:10.1300/J025v22n03_07

(b) to provide a medium for the students' voices to convey the importance they attach to this type of opportunity. Obviously, a critical point is the role science educators must play in creating computer-mediated curricular models that nurture a community of learners, both in the immediate classroom and beyond. *[Article copies available for a fee from The Haworth Document Delivery Service: 1-800-HAWORTH. E-mail address: <docdelivery@haworthpress.com> Website: <http://www.HaworthPress.com>*

KEYWORDS. Bioinformatics, Biology Student Workbench, biotechnology, critical thinking, problem-based learning, scientific inquiry, Type II technology, virtual lab, visualization

This paper describes the use of advanced technologies in a high school biology classroom to enhance inquiry in traditional science curricula. Drawing upon two years' worth of data, it presents the research-practitioners' reflections about the impact of Type II technologies when integrated into science education at the secondary level. Over 200 students answered questions about the use of technology in the biology classroom. The numerous quotes that occur in this paper are representative of the overwhelming response in favor of using technology in the classroom. All students in the program were exposed to the various types of technology that are discussed in this paper. There was no control group that was taught without the technologies. Quantitative data were not collected, but test scores have improved significantly.

The goal of this paper is to: (a) demonstrate the effectiveness of Type II applications of technology in creating an environment that allows students to be scientists in their own classroom, and (b) provide a forum for students to convey the importance they attach to this type of opportunity. Obviously, a critical point is the role science educators must play in creating computer-mediated curricular models that nurture a community of learners, both in the immediate classroom and beyond.

BACKGROUND: THE NATURE OF SCIENTIFIC INQUIRY IN THE CLASSROOM

If scientists were asked, many might recall the moment when they first felt the thrill of scientific discovery during an inquiry into the unknown. That moment may have been when they received their first microscope and peered into a single drop of water. Or, perhaps it was after opening rocks on a slate pile and discovering traces of ancient life in the form of fossils. Carl Sagan, a famous scientist, once said, "Everybody starts out as a scientist. Every child has the scientist's sense of wonder and awe" (CSMEE, 1998, p. 1). Everyone experiences this feeling at some time, but for many that feeling is missing in science classes burdened with too much content and too little time for inquiry. John Glenn, former astronaut and chairman of the National Committee on Mathematics and Science Teaching for the 21st Century, raises concerns about instructional patterns that diminish inquiry in the science classroom:

> If the core of mathematics and science is about inquiry, then too many of today's mathematics and science classrooms come up short. Students are crippled by content limited to the "What?" They get only a little bit about the "How?" and not nearly enough about the "Why?" Missing almost entirely is "Why should I care?" (National Committee on Mathematics and Science Teaching for the 21st Century, 2000, p. 23)

The *National Science Education Standards* (1996) state that the first goal for school science is to educate students "to experience the richness and excitement of knowing about and understanding the natural world" (p. 13). Developing and sustaining this sense of excitement present teachers with both a challenge and an opportunity.

To meet this challenge in our biology classrooms, we first asked ourselves what type of students we wanted in science. We knew we did not want students who acquire all of their knowledge through textbooks. This might train our students to take tests, but not to learn critical science literacy. We also knew we did not want classrooms where the teacher is the provider of all knowledge (or at least the knowledge needed for an "A" on the test). We considered the next three goals of the *National Science Education Standards* (1996) that state that we need to educate students who are able to:

1. use appropriate scientific processes and principles in making personal decisions;
2. engage intelligently in public discourse and debate about matters of scientific and technological concern; and

3. increase their economic productivity through the use of the knowledge, understanding, and skills of the scientifically literate person in their careers. (p. 13)

After reflecting on these goals, we felt that the ultimate goal was to provide a learning environment in which students could feel like scientists in their own classrooms. This meant that our students would need to be involved in the acquisition of their scientific knowledge by–not only reading and writing about–but *actually doing* science. Furthermore, we would want them to share and present their new-found knowledge–not only with their classmates, but beyond–via the World Wide Web.

TYPE II TECHNOLOGY AND THE SCIENCE STUDENT

Assumptions about what technology can do in the classroom abound. However, the voices of our own students and our own experiences as those invested in the future of science education indicate that Type II applications of technology do support effective learning. The students in these technology-rich classrooms expressed the importance they attach to this type of opportunity.

We felt we could engage and empower students as scientists by providing them with the opportunity to learn valuable technological skills, to apply knowledge to solve science problems using real data, and to become involved in real-life science. Type II technology applications provide teachers and students with access to the very same tools that scientists use, thus making "available new and better ways of teaching" and learning (Maddux, Johnson, & Willis, 1997, p. 18). Through extensive use of Type II technology applications, we have created an environment in which students are engaging in scientific analysis, moving beyond imitation to being scientists themselves. Type II applications provide tools that allow students to visualize complex concepts, perform complicated procedures, use the tools of scientists, employ scientific databases with current information, research matters of scientific and technological concern, and present the results of their work. One of our students expressed the benefits of this opportunity:

> *I have a better feeling as to what real scientists do every day. It is easier to get a feel for the trial and error [of the] scientific process. It was also fun to know that we were using the same technology that scientists around the world are using. I learned a lot by applying my knowledge in new ways, and in new mediums.*

The *National Science Education Standards* state, "The relationship between science and technology is so close that any presentation of science without developing an understanding of technology would portray an inaccurate picture of science" (NRC, 1996, p. 190). Type II applications don't just make students feel like scientists, these applications also help develop the skills of a scientist by (a) empowering students to overcome anxieties they may have about using technology, (b) stimulating intellectual involvement, (c) supporting an environment where students have a natural investment in their own learning process, and (d) allowing students to accomplish original tasks through the application of knowledge gained using real data. Students are very aware of the importance of this:

> *Since technology is becoming a more integral part of our daily lives, using it in the classroom helps me to connect basic knowledge to what we are learning. It also makes certain things, like research, more efficient and more interesting. Projects have become easier as well. Technology is only going to become more and more prevalent in our lives, and applying the knowledge to our learning will prepare us well.*

VISUALIZING COMPLEX CONCEPTS

In the last 50 years, man has gone from discovering the molecular makeup of DNA to sequencing the entire human genome. The focus of biology has gone from the organism to molecules that make it up. This shift is difficult enough for adults with scientific training, but much more difficult for teenagers without the scientific background. Advances in computer graphics have brought visualizations of complex concepts into the classroom. We can now explore such complicated topics as the mechanisms of cellular membrane transport, DNA replication to transcription to translation, and the immune response of blood components. Not only has visualization made these concepts easier to understand, but also it makes learning more efficient and more interesting to most students. A search of the Internet provides numerous sources for animations depicting difficult processes and concepts. The students note enhanced understanding via visualization:

> *I like the online animations because they help tie very complicated things together. It helps me to see things in action in order to fully understand it.*

In order to facilitate this type of understanding, we have collaboratively created online study guides for our honors biology students. Students may go to the study guide and access pre-selected visualizations. In this manner, students are sure to find material that is appropriate to their level of understanding, and they do not have to wade through the masses of material that come with most search engines. Students have control over how much material they need to view and when they need to view it. A student who used the Web site for this purpose said:

> *For a visual learner like me, the animations on the Web site help more than reading a textbook ever could. They allow me to be taught at my own pace with as many repetitions as I need.*

For more difficult topics, these visualizations can be used in class for discussions. Watching the visualization several times in the context of the classroom supports students' growing observation and inference skills. We often noted how this collaborative activity created a learning community, where students helped one another rather than competed for the "right" answer.

Technology in the hands of the students can also help them create their own visualizations. A good example of this is a project our students create on the cell unit. Students are asked to create a "cell theme park" in which the organelles of a cell become the elements of the theme park. For example, a food court may become a chloroplast, a roller coaster may become the endoplasmic reticulum, and the admissions area acts as the cell membrane. Students use technology to design a brochure or Web site that will entice people to visit their park, and in the process they understand to a greater extent the content of that unit (the components of a cell and their functions) because the effects are very visual and they have a point of connection to the topic. Students also gain valuable skills by learning to use programs new to them such as Microsoft Publisher or FrontPage.

PERFORMING COMPLICATED PROCEDURES: THE VIRTUAL LAB

Type II applications of technology provide alternatives to paper-and-pencil work and physical laboratories. Virtual tutorials, modules, tours, and especially labs enhance our curriculum in several ways. Virtual activities encourage students to think and act like scientific researchers. For example, students have the opportunity to design and test their procedures, especially those with several variables. This is often not possible in a physical lab due to limited time and supplies. Virtual labs also provide a means for students to experience scientific work not feasible due to the expense involved. One such learning experience involves DNA sequencing techniques and their applications. This type of technology is not available in high school settings, but students can still experience it via the Internet. These types of opportunities led one student to comment:

> *It helped me because I was receiving an interactive, hands on method of learning, as opposed to just reading out of a textbook and imagining the results.*

Experiments that require several steps to complete can be difficult for some students to follow. By using virtual labs, we have been successful in giving students pre-lab experiences. It helps students better prepare for their time during the actual physical lab and reinforces techniques and information they will need to complete the lab productively.

> *The laptops give us virtual labs that prepare us for the real labs. So we don't make as many mistakes.*

> *Technology allows less work to be put into taking the measurements and more thought into interpreting their meaning.*

USING THE TOOLS OF SCIENTISTS

Biology, especially biotechnology, has made revolutionary strides in recent years. Much of this success is due to the creation and use of technological tools. These tools are becoming part of everyday laboratory experiences in high school classrooms, because it is apparent how these advances will have an influence on everyone's life. Putting these tools in the hands of the students provides real-world science and allows students to experience the excitement scientists feel when they make discoveries.

Through biotechnology laboratory exercises, we have been able to help students apply biological processes to real-world problems. For example, DNA fingerprinting techniques expose students to real applications of science that take place in solving crimes, child custody issues, detection of genetic disorders, and personal identification. Other biotechnology labs introduce students to genetic engineering practices, such as recombinant DNA, whereby students manipulate bacterial DNA with a glowing firefly gene. Experiments like these spark student interest in applying this technology to the agricultural and livestock industry, gene therapy, and production of useful proteins such as insulin.

> *Using technology can help apply Science to the world I am living in. Sometimes I wonder when any of the stuff we are learning is ever being used, and when we do labs like DNA fingerprinting I understand that Biology is being used almost every time there is a crime scene investigation. It also helps clarify any unclear topics that I didn't quite understand fully.*

The use of biotechnology has also expanded our evolution curriculum by allowing us to move away from lecture and paper activities to actual wet labs. Protein electrophoresis techniques give students the opportunity to determine the evolutionary relationships among different organisms. Through an inquiry-based approach, students compare muscle proteins of fish and construct phylogenetic trees from their own laboratory results. Students have the opportunity to analyze evolutionary history and make predictions of structure-function relationships of proteins. The use of a thermocycler and polymerase chain reaction (PCR) techniques help students expand their knowledge about mechanisms of evolution. For example, students examine genotypic frequencies among classmates using the Hardy-Weinberg principle. Students think of themselves as scientists because they extract their own mitochondrial DNA, amplify it, use gel-electrophoresis, and then analyze their data to fit evolutionary concepts.

> *First of all, its hands on work. Instead of us sitting and listening to a teacher talk about it, we actually do the work ourselves and get involved in the technology. Secondly, it prepares us for the future when we will grow up and have jobs on our own that require a lot of technology.*

Computer programs that interface with electronic equipment are useful tools for gathering and analyzing information for otherwise difficult labs. We use the PASCO sensors accompanied with Data Studio software to allow the students to experiment in areas such as anaerobic cellular respiration, photosynthesis, and the energy content of foods. The difficulty of these topics for biology students without the background of a chemistry course has been made more manageable through the use of such equipment. Students are better able to visualize the biochemical reactions (reactants and products) by gathering data quickly and efficiently. Some types of data, such as oxygen concentration and pressure of produced carbon dioxide, cannot be gathered without this technology. Students are also able to view data tables and graphs simultaneously while collecting the data. The graphing software has a variety of supportive tools that allow students to focus on the underlying science without using valuable class time for data representation details. It makes it possible to collect, store, analyze, and present data in ways not normally possible with conventional classroom resources.

> *We are using technology that professionals use so it seems as though we are near their level of thinking.*

> *Using technology in the classroom makes biology more applicable to real life. When we use technology, we're simulating the work of real scientists, not just doing a paper lab where the outcome is already known.*

EMPLOYING SCIENTIFIC DATABASES: BIOINFORMATICS AND BSW

> Biology is increasingly becoming an "information-driven" science. In this view, biological research involves constructing meaning using the vast amounts of information compiled from experiments in the laboratory and observations in the field. The application of information technology to molecular biology research has created a new discipline, *bioinformatics*. (Harnisch, Comstock, Thakkar, Moore, Bruce, Jakobsson, Abbott, & Gabric, 2003, p. 2907)

The development of sophisticated tools to access and manipulate genomic databases has created the opportunity to develop the inquiry mindset necessary for effective teaching and learning. It has also provided the thread that ties our units of studies together. It connects the study of biochemistry, DNA, proteins, cellular functioning, genetics, and evolution. The National Center for Supercomputing Applications

(NCSA) has designed a student interface to a rich bioinformatics tool called Biology Student Workbench (BSW; http://peptide.ncsa.uiuc.edu/) that makes maneuvering through sequence databases more intuitive. Using the tools provided by BSW, students not only have access to and the ability to manipulate real data, but also have the opportunity to apply these applications in independent problem-solving activities. The integration of BSW into the curriculum actively engages students in the process of learning; and the use of active learning strategies promotes more effective learning (Jones, Valdez, Nowakowski, & Rasmussen, 1994). It is evident from student comments that this tool helped students find the connections among the topics we studied:

> *Without Biology Workbench, I would have never really understood what a complete genome sequence is, how evolutionary trees work, etc. With Biology Workbench, it allowed me to learn what the power of science can do not to mention the time spent just to come up with one sequence. It also showed me how the DNA was translated into RNA, and then into a protein. For our evolutionary project, it was extremely helpful to be able to go on Biology Workbench and search for the DNA sequences of certain animals.*

The use of BSW's visualization features also provided that thread that permitted students to see that the many units covered in class were all interrelated. In the past, most students had viewed these topics as individual chapters in a book; discrete pieces with no connections one to the other, much less to real life. Students study the cell, get their test grade, and then forget the material. Using technology and bioinformatics supported meaningful molecular and cellular connections for many students because subsequent activities required use of previously learned knowledge.

> *Biology Workbench opens up the whole world of science information to anyone. It has helped me understand things that a textbook would never do and what goes beyond the classroom. Information used there has helped me finish projects and study for tests. The concepts in the classroom can be made clear at the click of a mouse.*

CRITICAL THINKING AND REAL SCIENCE WITH BSW

One of the major goals of integrating bioinformatics and BSW into the classroom was not only to expose students directly to what research scientists are doing, but to engage them in the complex critical thinking that scientific research requires in today's technology-oriented world. Students feel as if the schoolwork they do has meaning. In addition, the technology makes them feel more like real scientists by promoting the application of their knowledge to research. Other benefits, such as enhanced creativity and just plain having fun with the projects, are also evident in our classes that have used these technologies.

> *It does make you feel like you are doing actual experiments because once you test a piece of information on it, you get actual results. This helps me understand that what we do in the classroom has an actual purpose and isn't just busy work.*

RESEARCHING MATTERS OF SCIENTIFIC AND TECHNOLOGICAL CONCERN

Technology is a valuable tool in implementing problem-based learning (PBL). Through these activities, students learn how to be scientists because they learn the processes involved in establishing conceptual models for understanding. In other words, they begin to understand *process*. In order for these activities to be effective, students must make use of research skills that enable them to solve problems. The Internet provides students with information from which to draw background material, and teaches them critical information literacy skills such as evaluation and assessment. It also allows us, as educators, to naturally incorporate "just in time" learning when we discover that we need to provide some additional information in an underdeveloped content area.

Core information literacy is particularly evident in several of our PBL activities. For example, to conclude our human physiology unit of systems, we have students participate in a PBL activity that requires students to learn the nervous and reproductive systems. In cooperative groups, students are given a medical file and asked to diagnose the problem, report causes of the disorder, and provide treatment options for the patient. The Internet provides students the ability to clearly research all aspects of the problem and to formulate facts and opinions on their own. Another research-based assignment requires students to determine the DNA and amino acid sequence that should occur in humans, the mutated DNA and amino acid sequence that occurs in the disease state, the inheritance pattern, symptoms, and prognosis. Electronic database information makes information available, such as that of genomics, which students would not have access to otherwise. These and other exercises increase student research skills, give them ownership of their work, and help students to formulate their own conclusions.

In today's scientific and technology communities, discoveries are being shared increasingly via electronic publishing, and being responded to by professional peers via Web boards and scientific blogs. In order for students to understand this growing sphere of knowledge, we have implemented a "current events" assignment. Students use the Internet to find articles about current science practices and research. They are required to find this information from reputable sources, summarize what they've read, and form their own opinions or reactions to the information. These articles often lead to stimulating classroom discussions about "hot topics" in the news involving science.

> *Technology is the future, and what better way to learn science, specifically biology, than using computers to access what scientists have written on the Internet.*

PRESENTING STUDENT RESEARCH

While using technology to experiment, gather data, and research topics of scientific concern has proven particularly powerful for our students, part of what we felt was using technology to its full potential was the sharing of knowledge among learners by publishing student research online.

By expecting students to publish their research online, a number of positive outcomes occurred. Students shared their skills with one another. They would help each other with the Web-building process, the writing process, data gathering, and data analysis. Depending on the situation, they may be in the role of teacher or learner. Sharing information in this manner between students created a new learning community that had not existed before.

> *The Websites we made using Biology Workbench really made us research hard and think about what was going on. This really helped us understand and learn a lot.*

PROBLEMS AND SOLUTIONS

As with any educational approach, the use of technology in our classrooms has its potential problems and concerns. The limited number of computers for classroom use at any one time is the major problem we encounter. The lower the student-to-computer ratio, the more likely students will be on task. To tackle this issue, our school has laptops on portable carts that can be used throughout the school. However, this takes advanced planning by the teacher. Also, decreasing this ratio encourages students to use the technologies themselves rather than relying on fellow classmates. A difficulty that arises due to a large number of classes using a few computers is an increase in hardware problems. For example, a teacher may open a cart and find computer vandalism and/or unreported malfunctions. Also, older computers may not support some new programs. The solution is expensive and requires in-house technical support sufficient for the number of computers, a recurring replacement policy for hardware, and installation of a schoolwide wireless network. Software must be updated to maintain its usefulness, but we suggest caution with updating too frequently as it may cause other problems.

Another major concern of subject specific teachers is that they are not technology teachers. For teachers to integrate technology, they require training on both hardware and software and released time to revise curricula in order to take advantage of the technological tools available. Classroom time constraints caused by teaching use of the technology versus content must be considered when deciding whether to use technology. Some students have a "cut-and-paste" mentality and, therefore, plagiarism must be addressed. Lastly, we use a wide variety of technological tools due to the advanced ability of our students. In lower level classes, we use fewer tools more often for purposes of familiarity and comfort. For the regular and low-level students, programs and hardware should be user friendly and more intuitive.

CONCLUSION

In the end, what seems to be most important is creating an environment that promotes inquiry type learning. It is more important than covering immense amounts of content. If covering content is our only goal and the spirit of inquiry is suppressed in our students, then who will be the scientists of tomorrow? Inquiry is science in its purest form. That journey into the unknown that comes with inquiry is what draws us to science. It is what lures scientists into years and years of research despite the obstacles. Type II applications of technology can help teachers create an inquiry-oriented environment.

From working with other teachers, we have observed that it is often the fear of technology itself or, the concern that teaching the technology will leave less time to cover the content, that holds teachers back. And yet the *National Science Education Standards* have provided teachers with the encouragement and guidelines to incorporate technology and provide this type of learning environment.

> The standards have, in turn, yielded a widely endorsed set of specific goals, such as the following: (1) students should learn science and mathematics as active processes focused on a limited number of concepts, (2) curricula should stress understanding, reasoning, and problem solving rather than memorization of facts, terminology, and algorithms, and (3) teachers should engage students in meaningful activities that regularly and effectively employ calculators, computers, and other tools in the course of instruction. (The Learning Curve, 1996, p. 13)

But national standards and goals don't enter the classroom each day and face a roomful of students. As teachers, we have learned from the data available to us from students' comments. Repeatedly, students voice the opinion that they want to use the available technology and they want to feel like scientists and perform experiments. Technology used to its fullest potential as a Type II application can help provide that environment.

We suggest that one solution to the quandary of "content versus inquiry" will probably be to fight for a reduced curricular scope, teach the content expeditiously, and squeeze in as much inquiry as time allows. However, another solution may be to simply step away from the dichotomy of "inquiry versus content," and instead consider the natural theoretical underpinnings of science as a guide for what we do in our classrooms. We need to draw on the strength of our own communities of practice, the National Science Teachers Association and the American Association for the Advancement of Science for instance, for support. We also can turn to our own students' voices, which are clearly telling us what works and what does not. They are, after all, the next-generation learners. It is our responsibility to proactively be the next-generation teachers.

REFERENCES

Center for Science, Mathematics, and Engineering Education (CSMEE). (1998). *Every child a scientist: Achieving scientific literacy for all.* Washington, DC: National Academy Press.

Division of Research, Evaluation and Communication, Directorate for Education and Human Resources. (1996). *The learning curve: What we are discovering about U.S. science and mathematics education.* Edited by Larry E. Suter. Washington, DC: National Science Foundation (NSF 96-53).

Harnisch, D. L., Comstock, S. L., Thakkar, U., Moore, S., Bruce, B. C., Jakobsson, E. J., Abbott, G., & Gabric, K. M. (2003). *Scientists becoming teachers: Lessons learned from teacher partnerships.* Society for Information Technology and Teacher Education International Conference, Issue. 1, pp. 2902-2908.

Jones, B. F., Valdez, G., Nowakowski, J., & Rasmussen, C. (1994). *Designing learning and technology for education reform.* Oak Brook, IL: North Central Regional Educational Laboratory.

Maddux, C. D., Johnson, D. L., & Willis, J. W. (1997). *Educational computing: Learning with tomorrow's technologies* (2nd ed.). Boston: Allyn & Bacon.

National Commission on Mathematics and Science Teaching for the Twenty-First Century. (2000). *Before it's too late: A report to the nation from the Commission on Mathematics and Science Teaching for the Twenty-First Century.* Washington, DC: U.S. Department of Education.

National Research Council. (1996). *National science education standards.* Washington, DC: National Academy Press.

Mahnaz Moallem
Hengameh Kermani
Sue-jen Chen

Handheld, Wireless Computers: Can They Improve Learning and Instruction?

SUMMARY. Reports show that handheld, wireless computers, once used by business professionals to keep track of appointments, contacts, e-mail, and the Internet, have found their way into classrooms and schools across the United States. However, there has not been much systematic research to investigate the effects of these new technology tools on student attitude and learning outcomes, nor has there been much research evidencing that handheld, wireless computers can improve student engagement in the learning process. The purpose of this paper is to use the literature on principles of learning and instruction to develop an

MAHNAZ MOALLEM is Associate Professor, University of North Carolina at Wilmington, Watson School of Education, Department of Specialty Studies, Wilmington, NC 28403 (E-mail: moallemm@uncw.edu).
HENGAMEH KERMANI is Associate Professor, University of North Carolina at Wilmington, Watson School of Education, Department of Specialty Studies, Wilmington, NC 28403 (E-mail: kermanih@uncw.edu).
SUE-JEN CHEN is Assistant Professor, University of North Carolina at Wilmington, Watson School of Education, Department of Specialty Studies, Wilmington, NC 28403 (E-mail: chensj@uncw.edu).

[Haworth co-indexing entry note]: "Handheld, Wireless Computers: Can They Improve Learning and Instruction?" Moallem, Mahnaz, Hengameh Kermani, and Sue-jen Chen. Co-published simultaneously in *Computers in the Schools* (The Haworth Press, Inc.) Vol. 22, No. 3/4, 2005, pp. 93-106; and: *Classroom Integration of Type II Uses of Technology in Education* (ed: Cleborne D. Maddux, and D. LaMont Johnson) The Haworth Press, Inc., 2005, pp. 93-106. Single or multiple copies of this article are available for a fee from The Haworth Document Delivery Service [1-800-HAWORTH, 9:00 a.m. - 5:00 p.m. (EST). E-mail address: docdelivery@haworthpress.com].

Available online at http://www.haworthpress.com/web/CITS

doi:10.1300/J025v22n03_08

action-instructional model for utilization of handheld computers in the classroom. It will explain how such a model was used to integrate handheld, wireless computers in the design and development of classroom instruction and what the evaluation results are. The paper also provides some insights on what was learned from this experiment.

KEYWORDS. Handheld wireless computers, computers, learning and instruction, handheld computers in classrooms

Handheld wireless computers (HWCs), once used primarily by business professionals to keep track of appointments, contacts, e-mail, and the Internet, have found their way into classrooms and schools across the United States. It is difficult to determine the exact number of HWCs used in schools nationwide and the way they have been used to improve teaching and learning, simply because the technology is still new in education. Moreover, schools that have adopted HWCs (PDAs) have done so without the benefit of research to guide them. The fact that there is not much evidence to indicate how the use of these devices affects student achievement has not deterred schools and teachers from integrating them into their instruction. Presently, it appears that K-12 teachers are using HWCs primarily as an instructional tool to either involve students in meaningful learning activities or to manage classroom assignments and student behavior. In higher education, HWCs are mainly used as: (a) an assessment tool in which students can easily capture or access data when they need it, (b) a tool to bring pedagogical changes to the large university classrooms by improving student-faculty interaction, and (c) an access point to receive and send personal and academic information easily, anytime anywhere.

The purpose of this paper is to use the literature on principles of learning and instruction to develop an action-instructional model for use of handheld computers in the classroom.

INVESTIGATING THE EFFECTIVENESS OF HWCs

Recently, the researchers received a U.S. Department of Education grant, Preparing Tomorrow's Teachers to Use Technology (PT3), to explore the use of PDAs for improvement in assessment of student learning in classrooms. To accomplish the program's goals, the school purchased two classroom sets of Hewlett-Packard HWCs (Jornadas) and a classroom set of Palm HWCs. A research project was also initiated to study the effectiveness of HWCs for improvement of university instruction, student attitude, and student learning.

Developing a design model was the first task. The point was not to investigate whether a specific use of HWCs is instructionally effective. Rather, the goal was to identify how and in what ways we could use this new technology to apply research-based principles of good instruction or conditions of learning to improve student performance. In other words, we came to the realization that on the basis of previous research, we should develop a list of principles of good instruction or learning conditions, and then use this list as a guide to identify how HWCs may facilitate the application of these principles.

USING A NEW TECHNOLOGY TOOL TO APPLY PEDAGOGY OF LEARNING AND INSTRUCTION

The literature on learning, cognition, and instruction is extensive. While this literature does not identify a universal best-teaching practice, one can find a number of key principles of learning and instruction underlying best practices (Bransford, Brown, & Cocking, 2000; Danielson, 1996; Merrill, 2002a; Spector, 2000). These key principles can be summarized as: (a) connectedness, (b) active learning, (c) feedback, (d) social interaction, (e) learning environment, (f) expectation, (g) self-monitoring or self-regulation, and (h) learning context.

On the basis of these core principles of learning, a similar list of principles can be established for good instruction (Merrill, 2002a). These principles are at the heart of fundamental and effective teaching and are shared by many instructional design theorists for good teaching practices (e.g., Bruner, 1966; Bransford et al., 2000; Gagne, 1985; Danielson, 1996):

1. create a well-managed learning environment;
2. develop and communicate clear expectations;
3. create a rich and well-organized physical setting where resources abound and are accessible to all students;
4. activate motivation and existing knowledge as a foundation for the new knowledge;

5. provide learning and assessment strategies that are appropriate for the type of new knowledge;
6. provide opportunities for diverse talents and ways of learning;
7. encourage active learner participation through activities, assignments and learning tasks, examples, and demonstrations, etc.;
8. develop reciprocity and cooperation among learners;
9. monitor learner performance and progress;
10. use discussions and questioning techniques to improve interaction between the teacher and learners;
11. provide prompt and formative feedback; and
12. encourage learner self-regulation and self-monitoring.

These core principles of learning and instruction were used to develop an Action Instructional Model for the project. The Action Instructional Model was conceptualized in terms of (a) instructional strategies or appropriate learning conditions (Gagne, 1985; Merrill, 2002a, 2002b) applied in preparation for instruction (*pre-instructional strategies*), (b) in actual delivery of new instructional materials (*instructional strategies*), and (c) in evaluation of instruction (*post-instructional strategies*).

The Action Instructional Model was then used as a framework to identify how HWCs can be used to provide such conditions for learning in a face-to-face university classroom. HWCs can facilitate immediate assessment of and access to student prior knowledge, motivation and learning, and cognitive styles through online and ongoing self-assessment tools. They can also be used to enhance self-regulation by providing individual student access to course materials and information prior to and during instruction, assisting students in their organization and management of assignments and activities, and by improving teacher-student communication of expectations. Student access to HWCs throughout the instruction also creates a resource-rich learning environment. HWCs can play an important role in presenting new instructional materials and improving teacher-student and student-student interaction during instruction. They provide immediate and ongoing access to teacher and classmate feedback throughout the instruction. Collaborative learning activities and problem-solving or application-based tasks are easier to conduct using HWCs due to immediate Internet access, possibility of onsite data gathering and analysis, file sharing, and peer assessment and editing during the completion of the activity. Eliciting individual student performance is easy and immediate through online testing and student-response systems using HWCs. Tracking and documenting student performance and assessment of instruction can become an integrated part of the instructional process rather than an extra effort on the part of the teacher and students.

IMPLEMENTING THE ACTION INSTRUCTIONAL MODEL USING HWCs

The strategies were used to design, develop, and evaluate two units of instruction for delivery of three different undergraduate education courses. A unit of instruction was defined as a minimum of two, one-hour and fifteen minutes classes for each course. A total of 65 seniors were enrolled in the courses. All three courses are required methods courses for undergraduate students who seek a bachelor's degree in education and teaching licensure.

Pre-Instructional Strategies

The following specific design strategies were integrated in each unit as pre instructional activities.

- Students completed an online, automatically scored learning and cognitive styles survey (Felder & Silverman, 1988) and a pre-test for each unit. The results of learning styles surveys were e-mailed to the instructor for his/her information about the individual learner.
- Students completed a graded individual assignment, specific to the content of each unit, which assessed their understanding of the reading materials. The expectation was that students would submit this assignment to the instructor using the Internet and HWCs prior to the instruction for the unit.

Delivery of New Instructional Materials

The following design specifications were integrated in the delivery of new instructional materials.

- To promote high levels of interactivity between teacher and students, assess student learning during delivery of instructional materials, and to provide immediate feedback, a Student Response System (SRS: a software that was developed by our computer science faculty) was used. Numina II SRS is a Web-based software that uses a combination of wireless networks, handheld computers, and a data projector to allow students to submit responses to questions posed by the instructor with the results displayed graphically in seconds for everyone to see. In preparation for the use of this interactive system during delivery of the new instructional materials, the instructors developed key questions related to the concepts covered in their lecture/demonstration or large group discussions.

- To create a collaborative learning environment and to promote active student participation, a problem-solving activity was designed for each unit. Students worked as a team to solve the problem or complete the activity, were expected to use Internet search if needed, shared files with their own team members and other teams, and assessed one another's responses.

Post-Instructional Strategies

The following design specifications were integrated in the post-instructional strategies.

- Students completed an online, automatically scored post-test for each unit. Instructors used student assessment of learning data (individual assignment, response to team activity, and pre- and post-test), observation of the student level of engagement in team activities and the SRS system to reflect on student understanding and delivery of instruction.

IMPLEMENTATION PROCEDURE

The instructors and the researchers collaborated in designing and developing the instructional materials for each unit, while the instructor for each course was solely responsible for providing the content. The researchers also developed a try-out session in order to train students and familiarize them with the implementation procedure. The try-out session emulated the implementation procedures and trained students in the use of HWCs for both taking online tests and assignments and responding to SRS. The handheld Jornada PCs was used in all three courses. The following summarizes the implementation process:

- At the beginning of the first class session for each unit, Jornadas were distributed to students. Students then were asked to connect to the Internet and log on to the WebCT site and complete a pre-test (quiz) that covered the objectives of each unit. Students were also encouraged to view the results of their test if the items were close-ended.
- Upon completion of the pre-test, the first class session proceeded with the instructor's lecture/demonstration and/or large group discussion. The instructor used the SRS (Numina II SRS) during his/her lecture to pose questions and receive feedback from students. The results of students' responses were projected as soon as they were submitted, both quantitatively (graphs) and qualitatively (students' narrative memos to support the yes/no, agree/disagree, true/false or multiple choice questions) and were followed by large group discussion.
- At the end of the first class, students received notification from the instructor for completing the unit's individual assignment (based on unit reading assignment) before the next class session by logging on to the WebCT course site. The instructor then reviewed students' responses to the individual assignment and provided individual and formative feedback (through e-mail or the WebCT course management system).
- The second class session began by distributing Jornadas to students and asking them to open a Word file that contained the team problem-solving activity. After a brief introduction from the instructor, students were grouped into teams to discuss the team activity and to compose a short report. The recorder of each team was expected to send his/her team's report to the instructor via e-mail and beam it (transmitting data wireless via Infrared) to the members of another team for peer feedback. Teams assessed one another's responses and beamed their comments back to the corresponding teams. Respectively, the instructor used the wireless system to receive the teams' responses/reports as they were submitted by each team through e-mail, to compile them in a Word file, and to project them on the screen for the large group discussion.
- At the end of the second session, students were given time to log on to the Internet using their Jornadas and complete the post-test. Students were encouraged to view the results and the elaborated feedback for both close-ended and open-ended test items. They were also asked to complete a print-based anonymous attitude survey at the end of unit 2.

EVALUATION STRATEGIES AND RESULTS

The formative evaluation focused on the following questions: (a) What happened when HWCs were used in delivering instruction? (b) What did students think about using HWCs in delivering instruction and which instructional strategies were found to be more useful from a student perspective? (c) What did instructors think about using HWCs during instruction and which instructional strategies were found to be more useful? (d) In what ways did using HWCs in delivering of instruction influence student learning and satisfaction?

Evaluation data were collected from four primary sources: (a) student performance on online tests (pre- and post-test), individual and team activities using records generated and kept in Jornadas; (b) student responses to an attitude survey (five-point Likert Scale) which measured students' general attitude toward using handheld computers and toward using HWCs for different instructional strategies; (c) instructors' survey and reflection notes on the student level of engagement in class activities and interactions; and (d) researchers' observational notes during implementation of the project. A combination quantitative/qualitative analysis was used to make sense of the evaluation data.

Evaluation Results and Discussion

What happened when HWCs were used in delivering instruction? Instructors' and researchers' reflection and observational notes indicated that in all three courses, using HWCs for delivering instruction changed the class dynamics from a primarily lecture-driven, large group discussion to a more interactive and student-involved learning environment. Instructors agreed that the applied instructional strategies using HWCs made them more responsive to students' understanding of the materials, helped students become more engaged during instruction, and encouraged students to participate more actively during discussion and team activities.

All three instructors indicated that prior and throughout the lessons they were worried about unexpected technical problems that could have occurred during the instruction. They also indicated that they were anxious about both classroom management issues and time. They were concerned about students' off-task activities and thought that it might take longer to complete the lesson using HWCs, given the design specifications for each unit. Even though all three instructors believed that their perception had changed by the end of the implementation of the project, this still created some discomfort and dependency on the presence of the researchers in the classroom, when HWCs were used. The instructors also noted that, if they did not have the researchers' technical and instructional support during the design and implementation of the project, they would not have agreed to participate in it. Another issue that was raised by the instructors was the time required for designing the unit.

Moreover, as noted in researchers' and instructors' observational notes, the use of HWCs during team activities improved the quality of student discussions. Instructors believed that this result was due to easy access to multiple online resources, file sharing and peer editing opportunity, as well as the process of displaying each team's response to the whole class for further discussion and elaboration.

What did students think about using HWCs in delivering of instruction and which instructional strategies were found to be more useful from a student perspective? The analysis of the student responses (N = 59) to the open-ended attitude survey item–"three activities that you liked the most and thought helped you in learning the course materials using a handheld"–showed that more than 76% of the students liked taking online pre- and post-tests because of immediate feedback and the possibility of knowing how much they knew before and how much they learned after instruction, 60% liked the Student Response System (SRS) due to its immediate feedback and anonymity of response, and more than 30% liked the file-sharing capability when using handheld computers. When students were asked to list three strategies that "you would use to integrate handhelds in your future instruction, assuming you had access to handheld devices in your classrooms," again, they listed online tests (63%), Student Response System (39%), and group activity (30%) as their choices. In response to "As a user of handheld computers and a prospective teacher who may use this technology in the future, comment on the issues that might have frustrated you during the use of the technology or you think may frustrate your future students," students listed the following issues: problem with wireless access (took a few times of trying to access the Internet) (44%), small screen and keyboard (27%), and learning curve with the technology (21%).

Analysis of responses to the attitude survey's close-ended questions showed that receiving immediate feedback through online tests and SRS influenced student learning. Students also felt HWCs created more interaction, enhanced their level of involvement during instruction, and increased their motivation by making the unit of instruction more interesting. Moreover, students thought using handheld computers provided good learning experiences and helped them better understand the lesson materials.

What did instructors think about using HWCs during instruction and which instructional strategies were found to be more useful? The analysis of the instructors' survey and reflection notes indicated that all three instructors thought that using HWCs to provide online pre- and post-test, to conduct team activity, and to facilitate interaction with students using SRS was very successful and helpful. They agreed or strongly agreed that all instructional strategies used for each unit were positively related to student involvement, level of participation, and learning of new materials. The following excerpts summarize some of the comments that instructors made regarding instructional strategies implemented during instruction using handheld computers.

> Using Jornada for team activities was very successful. Students were highly engaged and appeared to remain on task during the entire activity . . . *[instructor #1]*; Everyone in group was actively involved contributing to the activity . . . *[instructor #2]*; I think because students knew their team responses were going to be reported visually they attended more and elaborated a great deal. . . . During SRS students seem to be eager to participate and enter responses. I think the advantage for me was to hear from all rather than from a few . . . *[instructor #3]*; I think they [students] particularly liked observing the results of their responses in the bar graph. I think SRS enhanced participation and enthusiasm of my class discussion . . . *[instructor #1]*; I found the SRS being very stimulating for the students. There was high level of participation. Everyone responded to the questions and some provided good comments that help with further discussion . . . SRS also provided a good assessment of student understanding and misunderstanding . . . *[instructor #2]*; Pre- and post-test helped me assess student knowledge of the materials instead of making guesses . . . *[instructor #2]*; I had never used pre- and post-test in my university class before. It proved to be useful for my instruction. It also helped the students focus on the lesson better . . . I was surprised with the results of the pre-test indicating of my perception versus reality . . . *[instructor #1]*.

In addition, all three instructors indicated that the immediate feedback from students helped them in monitoring student learning and understanding their perceptions and/or misconceptions. The instructors also thought that having access to student understanding of the concepts during instruction assisted in tailoring the instruction toward student needs.

In what ways did using HWCs in delivering instruction influence student learning and satisfaction? Table 1 shows the analysis of student responses (those who completed both pre- and post-test in each unit) to pre- and post-tests for two units of instruction in three different methods courses for pre-service teachers. The analysis showed a significant difference (using a paired samples *t*-test) in student performance on pre- and post-tests, except for unit 1, a reading methods course for middle grades. The pre- and post-test questions consisted of a combination of multiple-choice and short answer items. Further analysis of instructors' reflection notes indicated that the result of the unit that did not show a significant difference was due to the misconception that the instructor had about student knowledge of the unit before instruction. Apparently, students knew more than what the instructor thought they knew about the unit given the results of the pre-test. However, since the lesson for the unit was already planned, the instructor did not have time to make major changes in the content of the instruction. Given the instructor's reflection notes, as a result of this experience she did make changes to the content of unit 2, which then showed a significant difference in student responses to both pre- and post-test.

Students' overall attitude and comfort level measured by five close-ended items in the attitude survey indicated that students felt positive about using HWCs during classroom instruction and that they enjoyed having an opportunity to use this new technology. In spite of the general positive student attitude toward the use of handheld computers,

TABLE 1. Analysis of Students' Responses to Pre- and Post-Tests for Two Units of Instruction in Three Different Methods Courses

Class	Special Ed.				Early Childhood				Middle Grade			
N	16				10				10			
Unit (Possible total points)	Unit 1 (60)		Unit 2 (60)		Unit 1 (50)		Unit 2 (50)		Unit 1 (100)		Unit 2 (100)	
Test	Pre	Post	Pre	Post	Pre	Post	Pre	Post	Pre	Post	Pre	Post
Mean	33.75	58.13	28.13	49.38	27	39	16.5	39	71	78	4	69
SD	12.04	4.03	9.11	9.98	4.22	6.58	6.26	5.68	11.97	13.98	5.16	21.83
df	15		15		9		9		9		9	
t-value	−8.46***		−8.30***		−5.31***		−9.0***		−1.17		−9.46***	

Note: *** < .001

about half of the students agreed with the items that asked whether using the handheld computers can be frustrating or difficult in the classroom. This result is consistent with the students' responses to the open-ended item that indicated that 44% of students became frustrated when the Internet connection was not as fast as they expected.

CONCLUSIONS

Several conclusions can be made based on the results of this project, with its focus on applying principles of good instruction to integrate the use of HWCs (new technology tool) in delivering instruction.

The literature review on how HWCs or PDAs are currently being used in public schools and higher education and the evaluation results of this project suggest that, as other researchers have noted, a premise for the use of HWCs is belief that they can transform classrooms to a learning environment in which problem solving, collaborative learning, and student involvement and participation are possible. In other words, the promise of handheld computers lies in facilitating the improvement of instruction. Both university faculty and school teachers need to be reminded that new and emerging technology tools such as PDAs are only effective if they are used to improve the process of learning and teaching that is established by research.

Faculty professional development effort should focus on helping teachers use good teaching practices to generate strategies for the use of handheld computers or any other new technology tool. School improvement plans that focus on use of technology for improvement of student achievement must also focus on good teaching practices as a foundation rather than trying to convince teachers that using technology makes the difference.

The project results also indicate that handheld computers can increase the quality of research-based, effective instructional strategies, such as student-instructor and student-student interaction, teacher questioning, real-world application activities, continuous assessment of student learning, immediate and formative feedback, and can also decrease the average time required to provide such strategies with more accuracy and higher quality.

However, as with other technology tools, learning how to use and how to integrate HWCs into instruction is not always easy for university faculty or classroom teachers. Faculty and teachers must have the opportunity to learn how HWCs can make their instruction better and easier. The results of this project suggest that traditional on-time faculty or teacher training workshops may not be effective in helping faculty or teachers to feel comfortable using handheld computers or to successfully integrate them into their teaching. A new approach that focuses on ongoing pedagogical and technical support from peers, mentors and experts might be more successful.

The use of HWCs in this project also points to an important value as compared with laptops. The project reinforces the fact that the value of handheld computers is not so much in their power as computers as it is in their small size and the fact that the student does not need a large space on his/her desk. Therefore, the real value is in the handheld computer's ability to improve the quality of student learning experiences by creating more communication and interaction among students and between students and instructors.

Observations made during this project imply the need for caution about a few management issues. One issue relates to the security of student and faculty information over wireless networks and the potential for classroom dishonesty should students decide to daisy-chain data to one another and beam answers from device to device. In other words, some of the characteristics that make HWCs attractive to classroom teachers may also present behavioral management challenges. To overcome these challenges, teachers need to have well-designed and properly-paced instruction to keep students on task and to prevent them from engaging in irrelevant activities.

In summary, as we welcome handheld technology into our classrooms and campuses, we should remember that, as with other technology tools, HWCs can only facilitate the process of learning and teaching. The primacy of teaching and learning is pedagogy, not technology itself. We should also remember that, although many types of applications are now available for handheld computers, and many more are in the developmental process, there is still much to learn about how HWCs may improve instruction and student performance. More research will need to be completed to systematically document the impact of these devices on students, teachers, and schools.

REFERENCES

Bransford, J. D., Brown, A. L., & Cocking, R. R. (Eds.) (1999). *How people learn: Brain, mind, experience, and school* (Expanded ed.). Washington, DC: National Academy Press. (ED436276). Also available online at http://www.nap.edu/openbook/0309070368/html/3.html

Bransford, J. D., Brown, A. L., & Cocking, R. R. (Eds.) (2000). *How people learn: Brain, mind, experience, and school* (Expanded Ed.). Washington, DC: National Academy Press. Also available online at http://www.nap.edu/openbook/0309070368/html/3.html

Bruner, J. (1966). *Toward a theory of instruction.* Cambridge, MA: Belknap Press of Harvard University Press.

Danielson, C. (1996). *Enhancing professional practice: A framework for teaching.* Alexandria, VA: Association for Supervision and Curriculum.

Felder, R., & Silverman, L. (1988). Learning and teaching styles in engineering education. *Engineering Education, 78*(7), 674-681.

Gagne, R. (1985). *The conditions of learning* (4th ed.). New York: Rinehart & Winston.

Jones, V. F., & Jones, L. S. (1995). *Comprehensive classroom management: Creating positive learning environments for all students.* Needham Heights, MA: Allyn & Bacon.

Merrill, M. D. (2002a). First principles of instruction. *Educational Technology Research and Development, 50*(3), 43-59.

Spector, M. J. (2000, April 28). *A philosophy of instructional design for the 21st century?* Paper Presented for the Structural Learning and Intelligent Systems, New Orleans, LA.

Kathleen Puckett

An Assistive Technology Toolkit: Type II Applications for Students with Mild Disabilities

SUMMARY. This article describes possibilities for technology use among students with mild disabilities. It considers characteristics of assistive technology from the standpoint of strategies associated with universal design for learning and Type I and Type II software applications. After a brief description of assistive technology definitions, legislation, and implementation issues, the assistive technology toolkit, an alternative strategy for equipping students with technology for classroom use, is presented. Observations from field-testing indicate that general and special education teachers can effectively use the toolkit to integrate general curriculum requirements for students with mild disabilities. *[Article copies available for a fee from The Haworth Document Delivery Service: 1-800-HAWORTH. E-mail address: <docdelivery@haworthpress.com> Website: <http://www.HaworthPress.com> © 2005 by The Haworth Press, Inc. All rights reserved.]*

KEYWORDS. Assistive technology toolkit, Type II computer tools, technology integration, mild disabilities, access to general curriculum, universal design for learning, teacher training

KATHLEEN PUCKETT is Associate Professor, College of Teacher Education and Leadership, Arizona State University at the West Campus, Phoenix, AZ 85069-7100 (E-mail: kathleen.puckett@asu.edu).

[Haworth co-indexing entry note]: "An Assistive Technology Toolkit: Type II Applications for Students with Mild Disabilities." Puckett, Kathleen. Co-published simultaneously in *Computers in the Schools* (The Haworth Press, Inc.) Vol. 22, No. 3/4, 2005, pp. 107-117; and: *Classroom Integration of Type II Uses of Technology in Education* (ed: Cleborne D. Maddux, and D. LaMont Johnson) The Haworth Press, Inc., 2005, pp. 107-117. Single or multiple copies of this article are available for a fee from The Haworth Document Delivery Service [1-800-HAWORTH, 9:00 a.m. - 5:00 p.m. (EST). E-mail address: docdelivery@haworthpress.com].

Available online at http://www.haworthpress.com/web/CITS

doi:10.1300/J025v22n03_09

Technology opens a world of possibilities for students with disabilities. By using technology, text that is perhaps poorly understood or not recognized can be read, defined, translated, captured, transformed, or linked to more information. Writing tasks, perhaps once blocked by physical, emotional, or expressive limitations, can be accomplished by speaking first, then editing with electronic tools. Attention and organizational skills, often the bane of active and creative minds, can be aided with organizational software and personal digital assistants. Technology can provide access, previously unattainable, to the content and processes of the general education curriculum for students with high-incidence or mild disabilities–those with learning disabilities, emotional/behavioral disorders, mild mental retardation, and developmental delays. This world of possibility for access to learning, however, has not yet been attained in our classrooms. Although continuing advances in technology applications offer the possibility, and legislative intents hold the promise, moving technology use to a world of reality will take concerted effort among teachers, students, and teacher educators.

As the educational benefits of technology for students with learning challenges are beginning to be well documented, assistive technology has an increasingly important role to play in helping special education students achieve general education outcomes (Anderson-Inman, 1999; Behrmann & Jerome, 2002; Fisher & Frey, 2001; Male, 2003; Rachow & Rachow, 2004; Rose & Meyer, 2002). Designing lessons with digital tools enhances the flexibility of the curriculum and increases the probability that all students will be able to participate in the learning experience, an element of planning referred to as universal design for learning (Rose, 2000; Rose & Meyer, 2000).

When technology is used to improve the performance of an individual with a disability, it is referred to as *assistive*. As software programs continue to advance in general usage, there is much less distinction between what is considered assistive and what is considered to be instructional. For example, an electronic dictionary, either on-screen or hand-held, may be considered technology that is a convenient reference tool, making the production of a written piece more efficient. That same electronic dictionary could be considered assistive technology when used by students whose physical, cognitive, or attention limitations preclude access to traditional paper-based resources. Similarly, software used to teach or reinforce academic skills in classrooms can also be used to help the learner achieve individual educational program (IEP) goals (Weber, Forgan, & Shoon, 2002). The terms *technology*, *assistive tech-*

nology, and *instructional technology* can often refer to the same software application.

THE PROMISE OF ASSISTIVE TECHNOLOGY: LEGISLATION REQUIRING CONSIDERATION

In the past several years legislation has increased the attention given to assistive technology (AT) devices and services for students with disabilities. The progress of all students, including those with disabilities, must be documented through the requirements of the No Child Left Behind Act (NCLB). The reauthorization of the Individuals with Disabilities Education Act (IDEA) clearly aligns special education with overall educational reform. Students with disabilities must have access, participate, and make progress in the regular classroom curriculum. Technology is cited as a necessary tool for implementing these requirements. When developing the Individual Educational Program (IEP) for students with disabilities, the IEP team shall "consider if assistive technology devices and services are required" (20 U.S.C. § 1414). An *assistive technology device* is defined as "any item, piece of equipment, or product system, whether acquired commercially off the shelf, modified, or customized, that is used to increase, maintain, or improve the functional capabilities of a child with a disability" (20 U.S.C. §1400(1)). Other initiatives, the Technology-Related Assistance for Individuals with Disabilities Act of 1988 and sections of NCLB, promote the use of assistive technology in home, work, and school environments.

TYPE I AND TYPE II APPLICATIONS

Because the definition of *assistive technology* is so broad, special educators generally refer to devices as being low-tech (devices such as pencil grips or highlighting tape) or high-tech, (devices that are computer based or utilize associated technologies). Since many computer-based assistive technology applications have characteristics similar to instructional software used in classrooms, the distinctions between the two begin to blur. Therefore, when considering assistive technology, it may be useful for a teacher to use the designations Type I and Type II when matching software applications with instructional goals (Maddux, Johnson, & Willis, 1997). Type I applications can be thought of as "closed" systems, developed to aid in the acquisition of curriculum-specific facts or skills. A Type I application could also be considered assistive technology. For example, a Type I application that is characteristic of many software programs used in special education classrooms is a drill-and-practice program requiring a specific, correct answer or response. When this software is used to achieve specific IEP goals, and when it presents information in multiple formats, such as text and voice, or provides flexibility in response modality, such as the option of using a touch screen or single switch, it may also be referred to as assistive. A *Type II application*, when the term is applied to assistive technology, would be considered to be software that is characteristically open, allowing an array of choices and control on the part of the user. Assistive technology that is used as a tool for access to unlimited content and expression with choices in levels of support, modality, and information access can be considered a Type II application. Examples of Type II assistive technology applications are scan-and-read programs and text-to-speech and voice-activated word processors.

CONSIDERING ASSISTIVE TECHNOLOGY: POSSIBILITIES AND REALITIES

Regulations developed by state and local school districts to meet the assistive technology requirements of IDEA usually require a lengthy process of referral and evaluation, which can take several months prior to the recommendation and purchasing of any device. Moreover, the referral and evaluation process usually results in the acquisition of devices designated for the exclusive use of that particular student. As a result, assistive technology seems to only be available for use by students with the most obvious needs. While this system may be appropriate for students with physical or sensory disabilities, the sheer number of students with mild disabilities resulting in academic and cognitive difficulties makes this form of consideration problematic (Edyburn, 2000). School districts are understandably reluctant to encourage technology exploration with special education students for fear that parents will demand evaluation, purchase, and exclusive use for that individual student (Schweder, 2002). The probability of a referral for assistive technology evaluation decreases when teachers of students with less obvious needs are not aware of possible applications.

All students with disabilities need more readily available access to assistive technology tools that provide instructional support. Given the large number of students with mild disabilities who could benefit from technology use in both inclusive and special environments, acquiring technology support and services using current procedures does not appear to be the most efficient way to consider the technology needs of students with mild disabilities, hindering the widespread use of assistive technology in special education. A proactive strategy, proposed by Edyburn (2000), would bypass referral for evaluation as the first step in assistive technology consideration, and would instead equip each classroom with basic technology toolkits that enhance teaching and learning. These kits would serve to "quickly deploy tools of obvious value into the hands of teachers and students" (p. 12) and provide readily accessible opportunities for exploratory use. The toolkit approach is organized around learner productivity tasks such as writing, reading, reference, math, study skills, and presentation strategies that are Type II applications and are adaptable to general education requirements. For example, tasks involving the mechanics of writing can be supported through the use of text-to-speech word processors, word-prediction programs, and/or alternate keyboards. Electronic concept-mapping programs support the cognitive and planning aspects of writing. Scan-and-read programs can support the reading process by converting text to digitized formats, making available such scaffolding support as screen reading, note taking, and reference tools such as definitions and synonyms (Behrmann & Jerome, 2002; Kaplan & Edyburn, 1998; Lewis, 1996; Male, 2003). Toolkits allow teachers to anticipate the support needed in inclusive settings to enhance learner productivity, and are chosen for features that meet a range of needs and abilities. Rather than following an individual student, these tools are associated with the academic task and therefore available when needed for support for many students. Advocates of the toolkit concept recommend further research in the process of development and use for students with mild disabilities (Edyburn, 2000). Researchers expect that as instructional technology continues to become more accessible, and as teachers learn to link technology use with curriculum design, the use of assistive technology applications as retrofitting devices will be much less necessary (Hitchcock, Meyer, Rose, & Jackson, 2002).

The assistive technology toolkit offered here is an organized collection of software and associated equipment that supports access to general curriculum materials and standards for students with mild disabilities. This toolkit was developed as part of an ongoing project intended to field-test its potential use in inclusive settings. General and special education teachers can use this toolkit to implement instructional practices that meet a full range of student needs. The toolkit is patterned around a collection of recommendations and reviews that matched classroom-based learning problems with core assistive technology and learner productivity concepts (Edyburn, 2000, 2003; Resource Directory, 2004; Zabala, 1995). It contains software, equipment, and strategies that support student achievement toward general education standards in math and language arts. Toolkit applications are content or curriculum neutral; that is, useable and adaptable as tools for supporting student achievement in curriculum standards without the use of pre-authored or drill-and-practice activities. Many of these applications could be used as either instructional or assistive technology, depending on the learning needs of the student. This toolkit is organized around assistive technology concepts that could be considered for specific learning problems. Table 1 presents the problems, assistive technology concepts, suggested resources, and product features.

The products listed in Table 1 were suggested based on ease of use and general availability. Other products not listed may have similar features and uses. A review of available products, features, and vendors is recommended prior to purchase (Resource Directory, 2004).

Observations from Field-Testing

The assistive technology toolkit was field-tested as part of a project investigating the integration of assistive technology applications with content and curriculum standards for students with disabilities (Puckett, 2002, 2004). Teams of general and special education teachers were trained in the use of this toolkit and were provided with representative software and equipment for their classrooms. The population of teachers participating was evenly distributed regarding age, number of years of teaching, number of degrees and certifications, and demographic area served. Although participation was voluntary and the number of participants was small (n = 70 over a three-year period), limiting the generalizability of these findings, several observations have emerged.

Curriculum Integration

Teachers are able to develop lessons that integrate assistive technology applications with general curriculum content and strategies in meaningful ways. Initial iteration of these examples of assistive technology integration, however, more resembled Type I applications. For example, the teachers used features of text-to-speech word processors or multimedia programs to develop what could be described as elec-

TABLE 1. An Assistive Technology Toolkit for Students with Mild Disabilities

When the Problem Is:	Consider This Technology Concept
Comprehension of text Difficulty organizing ideas for writing and reporting results	Concept mapping: Allows the teacher and the student to develop electronic concept maps in a variety of formats. Includes pictures, art, digital photos, and text to speech. Outline view interfaces with a word processor, providing a structure for writing or presentation activities. Suggested Resources: Kidspiration, Inspiration
Difficulty with reading, writing, spelling Need to simplify or modify worksheets	Text-to-speech word processors: Highlight text as it is typed or read: by letter, word, sentence, or combination. Provide writing support and auditory spell checks. Suggested Resources: Intellitalk III, Write: Outloud
Slow or limited key-boarding Word retrieval problems Difficulties with spelling	Word prediction: Offers choices of potential words after one or two keystrokes. Suggested Resources: Co:Writer, Intellitalk III, Text Help Read and Write, Kurzweil 3000
Need for visual or auditory presentation Limited expression due to reading and writing difficulties	Multimedia programs: Incorporate sound, pictures, text, graphics, and movies. Provide an alternate format for written expression. Suggested Resources: PowerPoint, Intellipics Studio, Intellimathics, Hyper Studio
Student can express ideas verbally but is limited in writing due to motor or perceptual difficulties	Voice recognition word processors: Transcribe voice directly into a word processor once voice is "trained." Suggested Resources: Dragon Naturally Speaking, Text Help Read and Write, MS Word (2003)
Difficulty with writing numerals Difficulty remembering algorithms for basic calculations	Electronic worksheets: Permit students to work out an algorithm on a computer screen. Unlike a calculator, the programs do not immediately reveal the correct answer. Suggested Resources: Math Pad and Math Pad Plus, Access to Math
English language learner Content area reading material is too difficult Listening skills which surpass reading ability	Scan and read programs: Permit books and other print media to be scanned and digitized using optical character recognition (OCR). Once digitized, text can be read, words can be defined or translated. Suggested Resources: Kurzweil 3000, Text Help Read and Write WYNN, CAST E-Reader
Limited access to word processing or need for portability; Lack of individual funds for computers; Poor organizational skills	Portable keyboards: Inexpensive, durable, portable method for keyboarding. Infrared or cable transfer to printer or computer. Some models have Personal Digital Assistant capacity. Suggested Resources: Alpha Smart, Dana
Keyboard access or the need to simplify keyboard input choices	Alternate keyboards: Membrane keyboard with variety of displays. Suggested Resources: Intellikeys

tronic worksheets–a question with a single, correct answer to be chosen among fixed alternatives. Subsequent discussions of the technology possibilities and purpose of the learning strategies produced curriculum examples resembling Type II application activities, giving students a more creative, open-ended assignment with attention to optional and built-in supports. These observations suggest a developmental process at work; as teachers became more familiar with the sophisticated capabilities of the software (a Type II characteristic), they were better able to conceive uses that supported development of higher order skills in students.

Assistive Technology and Technology Use

Unanticipated findings of field-testing were extremely low levels of knowledge and use of basic assistive technology applications obtained from participant self-reports prior to project activities. The teachers who field-tested the software entered the project with minimal awareness of assistive technology software and equipment, reporting limited knowledge of voice-activated word processors, text reading programs, word prediction, concept mapping, text-to-speech word processors, and alternate keyboards. Other basic technology skills were limited. The teachers had to be shown basic file management features, scanning procedures, and procedures to incorporate pictures from other sources. The only exceptions to these pre-project skills were in the areas of drill-and-practice programs and word processors, which were used frequently. These findings support the observations of other researchers concerned with levels of classroom use of technology and indicate a continuing need for technology training at both pre-service and in-service levels (Maddux, 2002; Cavanaugh, 2002; Vannatta & O'Bannon, 2002; ISTE, 2002; Lesar, 1998).

Access to Software

For the majority of the teachers, the software and equipment provided during the toolkit training was their first and only access to these assistive technology applications. This point did not go unnoticed in evaluation narratives; most expressed their appreciation not only for the training, but also for the immediate and unrestricted access to the applications for use with their students. These findings beg the question, How is it that teachers can become familiar with and use assistive technology if they have few opportunities for either training or use? The comments from these teachers are consistent with Edyburn's (2000) "paradox of consideration," a concern that teachers cannot consider the full range of assistive technology possibilities, as required by law, when they do not have the opportunity to access the knowledge base in this area. Implementation of a toolkit approach offers a potential solution to this concern.

IMPLICATIONS

The toolkit approach to assistive technology consideration can inform the field in advancing a common vision for assistive technology integration in classrooms, while serving the needs of students with mild disabilities who populate our classrooms today. In this NCLB era, it is unlikely that concerns for student achievement and access to the general education curriculum will diminish for this population. More than ever, teachers need ready access to available technology tools to assist in meeting student needs. The toolkit items presented here are easily available and can be obtained for a modest investment in funds.

The assistive technology toolkit promises access to the general education curriculum as it is currently configured. In an ideal world, technology offers infinitely more possibilities than mere access. In an ideal world, teachers and students would interact with a "universally designed" curriculum developed to reach the full range of students who are actually in our schools, including students with disabilities, rather than the narrow range of students in the middle that it now targets (Hitchcock & Stahl, 2003). In such an environment, students would have ready access to technology that enhances the curriculum. This technology would include items not unlike those presented in this toolkit. Moving technology use to a world of reality for all students, especially those with varying abilities and disabilities, is our ultimate goal.

REFERENCES

Anderson-Inman, L. (1999). Computer-based solutions for secondary students with learning disabilities: Emerging issues. *Reading & Writing Quarterly, 15*(3), 239-249.

Behrmann, M., & Jerome, M. K. (2002). *Assistive technology for students with mild disabilities: Update 2002*. ERIC Digest E623. (ERIC Document Reproduction Service No. ED 463595).

Cavanaugh, T. (2002). The need for assistive technology in educational technology. *Educational Technology Review, 10*(1). http://www.aace.org/pubs/etr/cavanaugh.cfm

Edyburn, D. (2003). Reading difficulties in the general education classroom: A taxonomy of text modification strategies. *Closing the Gap, 21*(6), 1, 10-13, 30.

Edyburn, D. L. (2000). Assistive technology and students with mild disabilities. *Focus on Exceptional Children, 32*(9), 1-23.

Fisher, D., & Frey, N. (2001). Access to the core curriculum: Critical ingredients for success. *Remedial and Special Education, 22*, 148-157.

Hitchcock, C., Meyer, A., Rose, D., & Jackson, R. (2002). Providing new access to the general curriculum: Universal design for learning. *Teaching Exceptional Children, 35*(2), 8-17.

Hitchcock, C., & Stahl, S. (2003). Assistive technology, universal design, universal design for learning: Improved learning opportunities. *Journal of Special Education Technology, 18*(4), 45-52

Individuals with Disabilities Education Act, 20 U.S.C. § 1400 *et seq.* (2000).

International Society for Technology in Education (ISTE). (2002). *National educational technology standards for teachers: Preparing teachers to use technology.* Eugene, OR: Author.

Kaplan, M. W., & Edyburn, D. L. (1998). Essential tools of the trade: An assistive technology specialist shares her tool kit. *Closing the Gap, 17*(3), 1, 8, 18, 24.

Lesar, S. (1998). Use of assistive technology with young children with disabilities: Current status and training needs. *Journal of Early Intervention, 21*(2), 146-159.

Lewis, R. (1996). *Enhancing the writing skills of students with learning disabilities through technology.* Funded project. Washington, DC: U.S. Department of Education, Office of Special Education Programs.

Maddux, C. (2002). The Web in education: A case of unrealized potential. *Computers in the Schools, 19*(1/2), 7-17.

Maddux, C., Johnson, D., & Willis, J. (2001). *Educational computing: Learning with tomorrow's technologies* (3rd ed). Boston: Allyn & Bacon.

Male, M. (2003). *Technology for inclusion: Meeting the special needs of all students* (4th ed). Boston: Allyn & Bacon.

No Child Left Behind Act of 2001, PL. 107-110: U.S. Statues at Large, 117 (2002).

Puckett, K. (2004). Project ACCESS: Field testing an assistive technology toolkit for students with mild disabilities. *Journal of Special Education Technology, 19(1)*, 5-17.

Puckett, K. (2002). *Project ACCESS: Accessing curriculum content for special education students* (Title II Teacher Quality Grant, PL 100-297). Knoxville: University of Tennessee.

Rachow, R., & Rachow, C. (2004). SKIP–Secondary Kurzweil Implementation Project. *Closing the Gap, 22*(6), 10-12, 23.

Resource Directory. (2004). *Closing the gap.* Henderson MN: Author.

Rose, D. (2000). Universal design for learning. *Journal of Special Education Technology, 15*(1), 67-70.

Rose, D., & Meyer, A. (2000). Universal design for individual differences. *Educational Leadership*, *58*(3), 39-43.

Rose, D., & Meyer, A. (2002). *Teaching every student in the digital age: Universal design for learning.* Alexandria, VA: Association for Supervision and Curriculum Development.

Schweder, W. (2002). New hardware, the wearable computer. *Journal of Special Education Technology*, *17*(3), 56-57.

Vannatta, R., & O'Bannon, B. (2002). Beginning to put the pieces together: A technology infusion model for teacher education. *Journal of Computing in Teacher Education*, *18*(4), 112-123.

Weber, R., Forgan, J., & Shoon, P. (2002). Software evaluation for special needs: Preparing the preservice teacher from an inservice perspective. *Teacher Education and Special Education*, *25*(4), 342-351.

Zabala, J. S. (1995). *The SETT framework: Critical areas to consider when making informed assistive technology decisions.* Houston, TX: Region IV Education Service Center. (ERIC Document Reproduction Service No. ED 381962).

Ann E. Barron
J. Christine Harmes
Kate Kemker

Authentic Instruction in Laptop Classrooms: Sample Lessons that Integrate Type II Applications

SUMMARY. Laptop computers and Type II applications can provide powerful tools for elementary classrooms, especially if they are combined with authentic instruction. This article provides information and lessons learned from a laptop initiative in an urban elementary school. The goal of the initiative was to develop lesson plans and document techniques that could be used to engage students in higher level thinking skills. Sample lessons are included to provide details related to the teacher's role, hardware, software, and student outcomes.

ANN E. BARRON is Professor, Instructional Technology, College of Education, University of South Florida, Tampa, FL 33620 (E-mail: Barron@tempest.coedu.usf.edu).
J. CHRISTINE HARMES is Assessment Consultant, Key Largo, FL 33037 (E-mail: harmes@earthlink.net).
KATE KEMKER is Educational Consultant, University of South Florida, Tampa, FL 33620 (E-mail: KateK@tempest.coedu.usf.edu).

[Haworth co-indexing entry note]: "Authentic Instruction in Laptop Classrooms: Sample Lessons that Integrate Type II Applications." Barron, Ann E., J. Christine Harmes, and Kate Kemker. Co-published simultaneously in *Computers in the Schools* (The Haworth Press, Inc.) Vol. 22, No. 3/4, 2005, pp. 119-130; and: *Classroom Integration of Type II Uses of Technology in Education* (ed: Cleborne D. Maddux, and D. LaMont Johnson) The Haworth Press, Inc., 2005, pp. 119-130. Single or multiple copies of this article are available for a fee from The Haworth Document Delivery Service [1-800-HAWORTH, 9:00 a.m. - 5:00 p.m. (EST). E-mail address: docdelivery@haworthpress.com].

Available online at http://www.haworthpress.com/web/CITS

doi:10.1300/J025v22n03_10

KEYWORDS. Laptops, ubiquitous technology, authentic instruction, sample lessons

According to Maddux, Johnson, and Willis, "Computers have the potential to become education's single most useful teaching and learning tool" (2001, p. 95). However, that potential cannot be reached unless the appropriate instructional strategies, hardware, and software are integrated into the learning process. This article presents sample lessons and classroom activities that combine three components–authentic instruction, Type II software applications, and laptop computers. Research related to each of these components has demonstrated increased student engagement and intellectual growth. Together, they form a solid, replicable formula for student success.

REVIEW OF THE LITERATURE

Authentic Instruction

Authentic instruction is based on the premise that students' work in the classroom should prepare them for the intellectual tasks that will be demanded of them as adults. In essence, authentic instruction "stands for intellectual accomplishments that are worthwhile, significant, and meaningful, such as those undertaken by successful adults" (Newmann, 1996, p. 23). In 1990, the U.S. Department of Education's Office of Educational Research and Improvement funded a five-year study on school restructuring to support authentic learning (Newmann & Wehlage, 1995; Newmann, 1996). The researchers visited over 60 schools across the country and observed students engaged in activities to create projects, compile portfolios, analyze data, etc. Based on their research, Newmann and Wehlage outlined three criteria that are consistent with authentic instruction: (a) Students construct meaning and produce knowledge, (b) students use disciplined inquiry to construct meaning, and (c) students aim their work toward production of discourse, products, and performances that have value or meaning beyond success in school (1993, p. 8).

Standards for Authentic Instruction

To help teachers assess the "authenticity" of classroom tasks and experiences, Newmann and Wehlage (1993) formulated five standards.

Each standard is considered a continuous construct, usually measured on a scale of 1 to 5. The standards are: (a) higher order thinking, (b) depth of knowledge, (c) connectedness to the world beyond the classroom, (d) substantive conversation, and (e) social support for student achievement. These standards are designed to "represent in a quantitative sense the degree of authentic instruction observed within discrete class periods" (Newmann & Wehlage, 1993, p. 11). The standards can be used as research tools or as a framework for teachers to plan and critique their goals, strategies, and outcomes. Newmann and Wehlage caution, however, that the standards are not exhaustive; there is no specific hierarchy of importance among the standards; and achieving a high level of performance on all standards in most lessons is "probably not possible" (1993, p. 11).

Type II Uses for Computers

There are many ways to classify the uses of computers in education. Taylor categorized classroom computers as tools, tutors, or tutees (1980); others refer to *learning with* computers and *learning from* computers (Jonassen & Reeves, 1996). Another classification has been presented by Maddux, Johnson, and Willis (2001) who describe computer applications as Type I (those that make it easier to teach in the same way) and Type II (those that enable new and improved ways to teach and learn).

There appears to be a natural link between authentic instruction and Type II applications. Consider, for example, the characteristics outlined by Maddux, Johnson, and Willis for Type II applications (2001, pp. 101-102):

1. Type II applications generally stimulate relatively active intellectual involvement on the part of the user.
2. With Type II applications, the user, rather than the software developer, is in charge of almost everything that happens.
3. In Type II applications, the user has a great deal of control over the interaction between user and machine, and the repertoire of acceptable user input is extensive.
4. Type II applications are usually aimed at accomplishing more creative tasks than are Type I applications.
5. With Type II applications, many hours of use are generally necessary for a user to discover everything a specific program is capable of doing.

Typical Type I software might include drill and practice, tutorials, and assessments. There are many examples of software that have Type II capabilities, including spreadsheets, word processors, databases, problem-solving software, telecommunications software, graphics programs, presentation software, and multimedia development tools. As Muir points out: "Within education, Type II applications make available new and better ways of educating students; innovation in teaching and learning. The challenge to us is to find those approaches" (2001, p. 2).

Research on Laptops in the Classroom

Even with an emphasis on authentic instruction and the availability of Type II software, it can be a challenge to effectively integrate computers in the classroom. In order to use computers as classroom tools, they must be available when they are needed–just like pencils and paper. Using laptop computers in a classroom is one way to address this issue.

With decreasing computer prices and the advent of wireless networks, laptops are becoming feasible options for schools. Several large-scale implementations, such as Microsoft's Anytime Anywhere Learning Program and Maine's Learning Technology Initiative, are taking place across the country (Cohen, 2002; Rockman *et al.*, 2003). In addition, smaller scale implementations can be seen in schools and districts in several states (Apple Learning Interchange, 2004; Lowther, Ross, & Morrison, 2001; Stevenson, 1999). Based on these initiatives, several research studies have been conducted to assess the educational benefits of laptops in the classroom. These studies have focused on motivation, writing skills, student achievement, absentee rates, perceptions, and other issues.

Of particular interest is the research related to using laptop computers to create student-centered environments. Rockman has published several research summaries related to Microsoft's Anytime Anywhere Learning Program (1998, 2000, 2003). The report for the third year of the study stated that: (a) Laptop students consistently show deeper and more flexible uses of technology than their non-laptop matched groups, (b) laptop teachers show significant movement toward constructivist teaching practices, and (c) for both groups, the large majority of teachers who indicated a change toward more constructivist pedagogy also indicated that computers played a role in that change.

In a study conducted with fifth- and sixth-grade students in Walled Lake Consolidated Schools (Tennessee), researchers sought to answer the following question: "Is teaching different in a laptop classroom?" (Lowther, Ross & Morrison, 2001, p. 3). The researchers conducted classroom observations in seven schools (four elementary and three middle). Their results showed, "In general, strategies promoting learner activity, such as cooperative learning, inquiry, sustained writing, and computer uses were more likely to be observed in laptop classrooms" (p. 5). They also noted significant differences in the following areas: (a) project-based learning (65% in laptop classrooms versus 22% in non-laptop classrooms), (b) independent inquiry/research (58% in laptop classrooms versus 24% in non-laptop classrooms), and (c) the use of computers as a learning tool (88% in laptop classrooms versus 17% in non-laptop classrooms).

CASE STUDY

In the 2001-2002 school year, the Florida Center for Instructional Technology collaborated with an urban elementary school to implement laptop computers in core curriculum areas. The goal of the project was to develop lesson plans and document techniques that could be used to engage students in higher level thinking skills and authentic instruction. This section provides information about the project, including the software, hardware, sample lessons, and lessons learned.

The Software

The selection of software is an important issue for laptop initiatives–the applications must be relatively easy to use, yet provide new and better ways to educate students. In this case study, several Type II applications were used, including graphic organizers (Inspiration and Kidspiration), spreadsheets (AppleWorks or Excel), and video-editing software (iMovie).

Graphic organizers. One of the Type II applications used in the classroom was a graphic organizer called Inspiration. This program allows students to organize their thoughts and visualize concept relationships using various symbols, words, or digital pictures that can be linked together in a variety of meaningful ways. This program is frequently used for brainstorming and mapping ideas. With Inspiration, students are able to use visual representations to clarify their thinking, communicate their ideas, or reinforce their understanding of a concept.

Spreadsheets. Spreadsheets, such as Excel or AppleWorks, provide tools for recording, analyzing, manipulating, and displaying data. They are versatile, require higher order thinking skills, and allow students to graphically display relationships to build and communicate concepts. In this project, spreadsheets were often used as a tool for students to visually interpret the data they created or collected. The elementary teachers involved in the project did not feel it was essential for the students to know how to create formulas, so they often embedded spreadsheets into a word-processing document. For example, the teachers would create a "digital document" for the students to use when gathering data. Students entered the data into specified cells in the document, and a visual representation then appeared as a graph in the lower portion of the document. With this approach, students could focus on analyzing and interpreting the data instead of entering formulas.

Video editing. Apple Computer's iMovie was also used with the elementary students. This Type II application is a powerful, easy-to-learn tool for editing digital video, sequencing still images, and incorporating audio tracks. Creating iMovies allowed students to be creative, while communicating information through a variety of media. iMovie is designed to be used with a digital video camera; however, in this project there were not enough video cameras or hard drive storage space to include full motion in individual projects. Instead, the teachers incorporated still pictures from a digital camera or from the Internet. This allowed more flexibility and required less time. While iMovie is rather intuitive, some direct instruction was required to acquaint students with the features.

The Hardware

Hardware was another important aspect of the success of the project. The use of mobile laptop computers along with appropriate digital devices such as scanners and digital cameras facilitated authentic learning and the effective use of Type II applications.

Laptop computers. If used with Type II applications, laptop computers can truly change the way teaching and learning occurs, both in and out of the classroom. The students are able to use the technology wherever they are located; they do not have to wait until they get to a lab or back to a classroom.

Digital devices. In addition to the wireless, laptop computers, other digital devices were key to the success of the authentic tasks. Scanners were used to create digital images of objects and existing photographs.

Digital still cameras were easy for elementary students to use, and they provided innovative means for the students to incorporate media into various projects. Digital video cameras allowed students to record motion video from which they could choose to use either the complete video or individual pieces, such as audio portions or still images.

Sample Lessons

Following are sample lessons in which Type II applications were used to create authentic instruction.

Ecosystem. In this example, students were studying about the ecosystem. The teacher created little one-foot plots of ground on both the sunny side of the school and the shady side of the school. Students were grouped into pairs and each pair was assigned a one-foot by one-foot plot of ground. They were instructed to count the number of living (such as plants and animals) and non-living (such as dirt and rocks) things, and enter their data into a spreadsheet. They did this for three days, examining a different plot each day. When they were finished with data collection, they created a bar graph from their data. They wrote a paragraph about each individual ecosystem and then wrote a paragraph comparing the different ecosystems. In addition to using spreadsheets to record and synthesize data, students also took examples of the living and non-living things they had found in the plots of land and scanned them to make digital images. As a culminating activity, students created a poster that included data, scanned pictures, and their written report.

This lesson would rate at the high end of the continuum for each of the five standards for authentic learning. It is particularly strong in the areas of higher order thinking and substantive conversation. Using cooperative learning, students worked together to gather data, synthesize their findings, and make judgments about their results. A high level of substantive conversation took place as students discussed their findings within their own groups in order to draw conclusions, and then with other groups looking for similarities and differences. Finally, they communicated their findings with the rest of the class through their reports and posters. The skills involved in this lesson have value beyond the classroom–hypothesizing, gathering data, synthesizing data to draw conclusions, working collaboratively to conduct research, using multiple types of input to create a report, and communicating findings with others.

Type II applications were central to this lesson, including spreadsheets, scanning software, and word processing. Students were actively involved in the use of the applications; they had control over the wide range of options, and they were engaged in creative tasks. Throughout the lesson, these Type II applications facilitated students' understanding of ecosystems.

Designing a luxury hotel. As part of a unit on fractions, fourth- and fifth-grade students used spreadsheets to design a luxury hotel. Within an Olympic thematic unit, students were tasked with designing a luxury hotel so that the most important visitors would have a place to stay. Students were given a grid template and a set of guidelines for designing the property. There were several elements that had to be included in their design, after which they were free to include other elements they thought their guests might enjoy, such as a pool or golf course. In the spreadsheet document, students highlighted the appropriate number of cells corresponding to the size of each piece of the hotel. They then used the paint tools to color each area separately (e.g., cells representing grass were colored green). After designing their hotel, students used a worksheet to calculate how much it would cost to build their hotel. They counted the number of cells they had designated for each area within the hotel, and made them into fractions representing a portion of the whole hotel. Then they reduced these fractions and converted them into decimals. They were given formulas for cost per square foot for building various elements within a hotel. Using these formulas, students calculated how much it would cost to build the hotel they had designed.

This lesson includes many real-world tasks. Relating these to the standards for authentic learning, it is especially strong in higher level thinking and shows strong connectedness beyond the classroom. In a problem-based setting, students worked together to analyze the situation, make decisions about elements to include in their hotels, and then made judgments about the impact of their decisions on the overall solution to the problem.

The spreadsheet, as a Type II application in this lesson, allowed for active intellectual involvement and creativity. Within a framework of the grid and guidelines, the students were in control of the input and output. The skills they developed (use of fractions, making decisions to stay within guidelines, visualizing fractions, working cooperatively to solve problems, etc.) could easily be applied in a multitude of situations.

Gettysburg Address. At the end of a unit on the Civil War, fourth-grade students used iMovie to create their own interpretation of the Gettysburg Address by working together to craft a multimedia production of this famous speech. The teacher grouped the students into pairs and assigned each group several lines to study and memorize. Students used a digital video camera to record each group reciting their part. The individual clips were then imported into iMovie, and the audio tracks were extracted. Students then downloaded copyright-free pictures from a Civil War Web site and imported them into their movie. They were tasked with selecting and sequencing an appropriate number of germane pictures to match the length and meaning of their audio portion. Each group produced their own iMovie, combining the pictures with the performance of their portion of the speech. Once each group had completed their movie, the individual movies were combined to create a single production of the entire Gettysburg Address.

This example of authentic instruction involved students operating at the higher end of the continuum of the five standards. Students were engaged in higher order thinking and developed deep knowledge by analyzing their portion of the speech, making judgments regarding the appropriate images to use in communicating their section, and synthesizing these elements into a complete package. This lesson also involved a high level of positive social support, as students worked together to build understanding, first in groups, and then as an entire class.

The multimedia production in this sample lesson exemplified the use of Type II applications in using technology as a tool to facilitate learning. Students used still images, digital video cameras, video editing software, and recorded audio to collaboratively create a product. They were actively engaged–choosing which pictures to use, how they performed their individual pieces of the address, and how these elements were woven together. They were using the applications as tools to create their own meaning, not responding to prompts from an application; they had control over the interaction, and the task encouraged creativity.

Cardinal directions in the classroom. A simple use of a Type II application, Kidspiration, was used to help primary students understand cardinal directions (a concept that is often difficult). In this lesson, the students opened a blank document in Kidspiration and labeled areas of the page with N, S, W, and E, to represent each of the cardinal directions. The students then went through the symbol library and selected pictures that represented actual objects in their classroom. They then placed these pictures in the appropriate area within the graphic organizer page corresponding to the cardinal direction.

Kidspiration allowed the students to develop cognitive skills with the visual recognition of symbols and their location in the classroom. Rather than have the students use a program with a pre-drawn classroom, the teacher wanted to make the lesson relevant to the students and their specific classroom. Labeling the directions with their initial letters reinforced letter recognition.

These sample lessons provide illustrations of how students can be actively engaged in authentic tasks and use Type II applications to learn with technology. The use of laptops provided the mobility and flexibility required for effective and efficient lessons.

Lessons Learned

Laptop computers and Type II applications are powerful tools; however, they can also present challenges for classroom management. This section provides a synopsis of a few of the "lessons learned" in this case study.

Standardize machines and store files on a network. The majority of students involved in this project did not have a computer at home, and did not have any concept of file structures or operating systems. Mobile carts were used in this project, and several classrooms took turns using the laptops. Thus, it was important to have a standard configuration for all of the laptops, so that it would not matter which laptop students received, and they did not have to become re-acquainted with a new computer each time. To facilitate file maintenance, a student server was set up with file folders for each student in the classroom.

Start with simple projects. It is common for teachers to have a great deal of enthusiasm at the beginning of an initiative like this one and to start by embarking on a very ambitious project. A better approach is to begin with simple lessons and projects that will allow both students and teachers to experience success quickly. As teachers and students become more familiar with the hardware and software, they can then tackle more complex tasks and projects.

Create mentors or "tech buddies." Since this school did not offer a computer class for the students, it became the role of the teacher to act as a computer specialist, troubleshooting technical issues and providing instruction on computer use. An effective solution was to encourage students to become technology "buddies" or mentors. Students who were especially adept or familiar with specific applications took responsibility for helping others who were having difficulty. This gave the teacher more freedom to concentrate on the curriculum.

Accommodate elementary students' cognitive and psychomotor skills. There were aspects of both the hardware and software that proved challenging for younger elementary students. Teachers found that students experienced frustration with drop-down menus–these menus are not intuitive and their use requires more advanced psychomotor skills, especially when using a trackpad. While the trackpad can be simple for an adult, it can be a physical challenge for some students. To accommodate this, teachers found that it was much more productive to use keyboard shortcuts.

Don't focus on the technology. When integrating laptop computers with Type II software, the teacher plays the role of communicating how the students will adopt the technology. In this case study, the teachers created an atmosphere wherein the laptop computers were treated like a book or any other tool used in the classroom.

CONCLUSION

The majority of teachers involved in this project were master teachers who created a culture of students constructing knowledge while engaged in authentic tasks. The combination of laptop computers and Type II software allowed the classroom to expand beyond the four walls and enabled learning to reach innovative levels. Based on reflections by the teachers and the principal and the level of engagement experienced by the students, the project was very successful. In their reflections, the teachers commented on how engaged the students became in the technology-enhanced lessons. Although the second-grade teachers were originally skeptical about giving a thousand dollar laptop to second-grade children, they were amazed at the outcome. When the computers were being used, the students did not sit quietly staring at the computer screen. Instead, they were on task and engaged in using the laptops as a tool to build critical thinking skills and create authentic projects. The principal commented that (during her classroom observations) it was impossible to distinguish students with learning disabilities or language barriers because all of the students were engaged in the curriculum.

The results of the project were used to develop a Web site with sample lessons and strategies. This Web site, titled "No Strings Attached" (Florida Center for Instructional Technology, 2004), provides dozens of sample lessons, each complete with lists of objectives, materials, relevant NETS competencies, extension activities, and templates. In addition, it offers practical classroom ideas, training tips, and reflections by teachers and students. This Web site is available to provide guidance for teachers who are considering implementation of mobile laptops in elementary school classrooms.

REFERENCES

Apple Learning Interchange. (2004). *Building a 21st century learning community: Manatee County, Florida.* Retrieved January 21, 2004, from http://ali.apple.com/ali_sites/ali/exhibits/1000884/.

Cohen, R. (2002, June 15). Laptops in Bar Harbor get high marks. *Bangor Daily News.* Retrieved January 19, 2004, from http://www.state.me.us/mlte/pressroom/articles/061502BDNCONNERS-EMERSON.htm.

Florida Center for Instructional Technology. (2004). *No strings attached!* Retrieved February 28, 2004, from http://etc.usf.edu/wireless.

Jonassen, D. H., & Reeves, T. C. (1996). Learning with technology: Using computers as cognitive tools. In D.H. Jonassen (Ed.), *Handbook of research for educational communications and technology* (pp. 693-719). New York: Macmillan.

Lowther, D., Ross, S. M., & Morrison, G. R. (2001). Evaluation of laptop program: Successes and recommendations. *National Educational Computing Conference Proceedings.* (ERIC Document Reproduction Service No. ED 462 937.)

Maddux, C. D., Johnson, D. L, & Willis, J. W. (2001). *Educational computing: Learning with tomorrow's technologies* (3rd ed.). Boston, MA: Allyn & Bacon.

Muir, M. (2001). *Integrating technology: Instructional designs for technology.* Maine Center for Meaningful Engaged Learning. Retrieved February 24, 2004, from http://www.mcmel.org/tech/InstDesign.html.

Newmann, F. M., & Wehlage, G. G. (1993, April). Five standards of authentic instruction. *Educational Leadership, 50*(7), 8-12.

Newmann, F.M. (1996). *Authentic achievement: Restructuring schools for intellectual quality.* San Francisco: Jossey-Bass.

Newmann, F. M., & Wehlage, G. G. (1995). *Successful school restructuring: A report to the public and educators.* Madison, WI: University of Wisconsin Education Center.

Rockman *et al.* (1998). Powerful tools for schooling: Second year study of the laptop program. San Francisco. Retrieved January 15, 2004, from http://rockman.com/projects/laptop.

Rockman *et al.* (2000). A more complex picture: Laptop use and impact in the context of changing home and school access. San Francisco. Retrieved January 15, 2004, from http://rockman.com/projects/laptop/laptop3exec.htm.

Rockman *et al.* (2003). Learning from laptops. *Threshold Magazine.* Retrieved January 15, 2004, from http://rockman.com/Articles.htm.

Stevenson, K. R. (1999). *Evaluation report –Year 3: Middle school laptop program.* Beaufort County School District: Beaufort, S.C. laptop project. Retrieved January 18, 2004, from http://www.beaufort.k12.sc.us/district/evalreport3.htm.

Taylor, R. P. (Ed.). (1980). *The computer in the school: Tutor, tool, tutee.* NY: Teachers College Press.

Candace Figg
Jenny Burson

Across the Curriculum with Handheld Computers

SUMMARY. Using computer technology to support authentic learning activities produces effective learning environments *when* two situations occur–the teacher understands how technology tools can be used in delivering instruction and the students have access to the tools anywhere and anytime. The use of handheld computers in classrooms hints at the possibility of providing computer access for every student in classrooms across the country; and with teachers developing a repertoire of activities based on activity structures designed to deliver instruction that seamlessly integrates technology into a variety of learning situations, students everywhere can participate in learning environments that support interactive, creative, and learner-centered scholarship. This article describes the use of activity structures to seamlessly integrate handheld computers into instructional designs that promote these types of learning environments.

CANDACE FIGG is Assistant Professor, Educational Instructional Design and Technology Program, West Texas State University, Canyon, TX 79016-0001 (E-mail: phd@figg.com).
JENNY BURSON is Lecturer, Curriculum and Instruction Department, University of Texas at Austin, TX 78712-1294 (E-mail: jburson@mail.utexas.edu).

[Haworth co-indexing entry note]: "Across the Curriculum with Handheld Computers." Figg, Candace, and Jenny Burson. Co-published simultaneously in *Computers in the Schools* (The Haworth Press, Inc.) Vol. 22, No. 3/4, 2005, pp. 131-144; and: *Classroom Integration of Type II Uses of Technology in Education* (ed: Cleborne D. Maddux, and D. LaMont Johnson) The Haworth Press, Inc., 2005, pp. 131-144. Single or multiple copies of this article are available for a fee from The Haworth Document Delivery Service [1-800-HAWORTH, 9:00 a.m. - 5:00 p.m. (EST). E-mail address: docdelivery@haworthpress.com].

Available online at http://www.haworthpress.com/web/CITS

doi:10.1300/J025v22n03_11

KEYWORDS. Handheld computers, technology integration, computers in the classroom, instructional technology, technological literacy, mobile technologies, portable technologies

ACCESS FOR ALL: EVERY STUDENT, EVERY SCHOOL

More powerful than the first desktop computers (when developed), more functionally agile than a graphing calculator, less expensive than a laptop, and more versatile than digital cameras, the handheld computer (HHC) may quickly become the ubiquitous classroom tool. HHCs of today are small enough to be added to backpacks and used at student desks. Small size and a simple interface, with peripherals that are often *plug and play*, have made the highly mobile device an interesting option for K-12 classrooms. But, more importantly, as of this writing, the price of a HHC with a built-in camera and audio recorder is under $250–much less than the price of a typical laptop computer that could offer the same portability–making HHCs an attractive alternative that can stretch technology budgets so that more students are given computer access.

The evolution of mobile technology from organizers to supermobile computers has led many educators to begin utilizing HHCs in their daily classroom instruction. The purpose of this discussion is to highlight effective strategies for teaching content with activities that seamlessly integrate HHCs with just-in-time technology.

Teaching with HHCs

Impacting student achievement with the integration of computer technologies into classroom instruction is dependent upon many factors. First and foremost, lack of access to computing tools at school and home has been cited as one of the largest obstacles impeding integration (Becker, 1994; Becker & Ravitz, 2001; Park & Staresina, 2004; Ringstaff & Kelley, 2002). As reported by SRI International in the most comprehensive study to date on the use of HHCs in the classroom, participant schools were able to provide more students with computer access by purchasing HHCs; and those schools distributing HHCs employing the "personal use" strategy, or allocating HHCs to students to use whenever and wherever they needed for a predetermined length of time–usually a semester or year distribution–observed an increase in "students' time spent on schoolwork outside of school time" as opposed to situations where schools provided "shared sets" of classroom HHCs, which were issued for use either on a daily or as-needed basis (SRI International, 2002, p. ii).

Teachers also cite time to teach the technology as an impediment to integrating technology into daily instructional uses (Hadley & Sheingold, 1993). However, teachers participating in the Palm Education Pioneers (PEP) evaluation study found that HHCs were "more easily integrated into the flow of learning activities than desktop computers" (SRI International, 2002, p. 7). A simple interface (along with the short learning curve required to master use) makes the HHC a readily available tool for teachers to use in instruction. In addition, building lesson designs utilizing "activity structures," or the frameworks/structures of activities that can be adapted to any content or grade level (Harris, 1998), that have been infused with small "bits" of technology skills, allows teachers to include technologically enhanced activities without spending large amounts of time teaching the *tools*, but are instead, teaching *with* the tools. With over 14,000 software applications available for Palm OS HHCs alone, implementation of these technologically enhanced activity structures is easily supported by handheld technology.

Although the barriers of integrating computer technologies into instruction, including access and time, can be addressed with HHCs, research has shown that student achievement is best impacted by computer technologies when the teacher integrates technology in a problem-based, performance assessment environment (CEO Forum on Education and Technology, 2001). Ninety percent of teachers participating in the PEP research felt that HHCs were a useful educational tool and that HHCs had the potential for making a positive impact on student learning. Even though HHCs were found to improve learning across most curricular activities, teachers indicated that one outstanding benefit was increased student collaboration (SRI International, 2002).

USING "TECHNOLOGICALLY ENHANCED" ACTIVITY STRUCTURES IN INSTRUCTIONAL DESIGN

Joyce, Weil, and Calhoun (2003) suggest that teachers must develop a repertoire of activities and understand how to sequence the structures in instructional designs for different learning outcomes, as well as adapt the designs to meet the learning needs of a diverse population of students. Activity structures that include components of computer technology should also be included in that repertoire.

These technologically enhanced activity structures include a component of just-in-time teaching (Rozycki, 1999). By breaking the teaching of technology skills into smaller, more manageable units that are then incorporated into an activity structure, students experience minimal "technology" instruction as an integral, authentic part of the learning–the student is required to *use* the technology in order to complete the learning activity. In addition, limiting the technology to a small "dose" requires only a few easily mastered skills while learning the content, and the technology becomes a seamless part of the instruction.

These short structured activities help students connect technology to familiar activities. For example, journaling is an activity structure that is used throughout many content areas and grade levels. Kindergartners "write" journals to record growth of seeds by drawing sketches, and ninth graders use journals to document the changes they see on a daily basis in the erosion of the soil on campus. Math journals help students reflect upon the learning process they use to solve problems (Roblyer, 2003), and predictive journals in science classes allow students to predict what they think will happen in the experiment they are about to conduct. Journaling is the framework of a learning activity.

However, journaling is just one activity within a sequence of activities to deliver the learning objective. Effective teaching uses the journaling as only part of the lesson instruction–never the whole instruction. Other activities are developed to build upon the learning outcomes of the previous activity. See Figure 1 for a seventh-grade science lesson that begins an investigation with a journaling activity and then incorporates other activity structures to complete an appropriate sequence of learning activities to deliver desired learning objectives.

The discussion that follows highlights activity structures that can be appropriately delivered with HHCs.

ACTIVITY STRUCTURES RELATED TO OBSERVATION, PREDICTION, RECORDING

The acts of observation, prediction, and recording are often activities that serve as the initial building blocks necessary to build conceptual knowledge or skills. In addition to journaling there are two other powerful activity structures that serve to promote these learning outcomes:

FIGURE 1. Example lesson plan that incorporates HHCs and activity structures.

The Urban Forest: Documenting the Forest in Our Local Habitat

LESSON OBJECTIVE:
The student will use appropriate tools and techniques to gather, analyze and interpret data needed to identify and classify trees native to the local environment (populations and ecosystems).

Memo 5 of 5
Unfiled
My favorite tree is the peace tree in my backyard. I was given the seed from a peach out of the yard of the President of the United States. My dad helped me plant the seed in a small pot and raise it until it was about 3 feet tall. Then, he helped me plant the tree in the ground. Now, we have blossoms each spring and peaches each summer!
Done
Details

FOCUS ACTIVITY:
Journaling: Students choose a favorite tree that has some meaning for them. Using the drawing software on the handheld computer (Sketchy, Teal Paint, or Sketcher), students will sketch a picture of the tree. Students will explain why this tree was chosen by recording their stories in a journal entry using Memos or QuickWord,. Students will read their stories and share their drawings with the class by using the Mirror application from Margi's Presenter-To-Go. Margi Mirror software allows users to project the current contents of the LCD screen of any handheld using a digital projector or VGA monitor.

DEVELOPMENTAL ACTIVITIES:
1) Digital Record: Students are placed in groups and assigned the task of identifying a specific tree on the school campus. Students use a field guide web page (that has been pulled down from the web using AvantGo and placed onto the handheld so that students can carry the information into the field). Based on their comparisons of the tree leaves, flowers, and/or seeds from their assigned tree to the field guide, students make an identification of their assigned tree. Students collect the following information for that tree into a HanDBase-3 database on their handhelds:

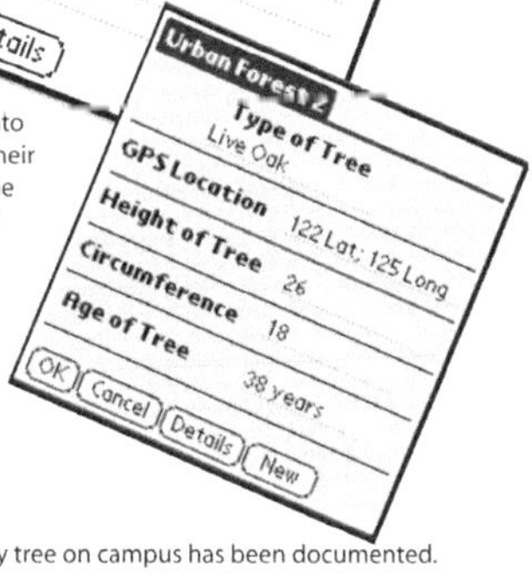

- GPS readings (latitude and longitude)
- Circumference of tree (using a loggers' tape)
- Height of tree (using a clinometer)
- Age of tree (calculated from core sample gathered from an increment borer). Students then take a digital picture of the tree with the digital camera that attaches to the handheld.

2) Digital Collection:
All trees identified by student groups are collected into one database so that every tree on campus has been documented. Students "beam" their records to one handheld so that all of the records are collected in one database. The compiled database is beamed back to the students for analysis and presentation of findings.

EVALUATION ACTIVITY:
Data Analysis: Students analyze data to create a map that depicts the Campus Forest. Using the compiled database that has been beamed back to their handhelds, students construct a map that details the campus forest. Students develop a legend that uses symbols to stand for the types of trees located on campus and place these symbols on a map using the GPS readings in the database. Labels also placed on the map identify height, size, and age of the trees.

Presentations: Students present their map to the rest of the class. (Although students may create their maps using many different mediums, we envision a map that is created in PowerPoint or some other program and saved as a graphic file. Both of these files can be downloaded to a handheld computer during synchronization and viewed using the Margi Mirror software that allows contents of the handheld computer screen to be displayed via LCD projector. Margi Presenter-To-Go software displays complete PowerPoint presentations.)

ASSESSMENT:
Students will be assessed using a rubric or checklist that lists components needed for successful completion of activity.

- *Creating diagrams:* When creating a journal entry, the recorder may find that an "image" is worth a thousand words! Then, the observational journal entry will include a diagram, picture, sketch, or some other type of visual to record the event. Sketches and other freehand drawings are created using draw/paint applications, such as TealPaint 6.37.
- *Creating digital records:* Digital pictures taken with a digital camera (such as those taken with the Zire 72 built-in camera) serve as a journal entry. Text that describes information about the digital image can be recorded as a note or as part of the image itself. A photo journal may be created by having students compose one entry that is compiled with other student journals to create a class journal, or the student may compose several entries to create a personal journal. (See http://www.figg.com/edt5555/photoessay1.ppt for an online example of a photo journal.)

ACTIVITY STRUCTURES RELATED TO PREWRITING, BRAINSTORMING, LISTING

Other initial activity structures that promote basic conceptual knowledge and skills incorporate the activities of prewriting, brainstorming, and listing. These activities serve to promote skills in classifying and categorizing.

For example, by repurposing Memos/Tasks applications or using a word-processing application like QuickWord, students are able to jot down ideas quickly when working on brainstorming or listing activities. Another approach might be to organize the brainstorming activity with outlining software such as Inspiration. The advantage of using the HHC for brainstorming and listing rather than the traditional pencil-and-paper method is that it allows for quick and easy reorganization of ideas. An additional bonus is that the files created can be transferred via beaming to other HHCs or synchronized to desktop computers. Other students can review and discuss ideas based on the shared files.

The following activity structures are two other powerful means of promoting similar learning outcomes:

- *Constructing concept maps:* In a concept map, two or more concepts are linked by words that describe their relationship. Concept maps allow students to take new information and organize new ideas into their existing body of knowledge. Inspiration is a tool that allows students to create a map of the subtopics and sub-subtopics related to an idea. These topics are all connected with word labels to further explain the relationship.

- *Animating ideas:* Relationships for many concepts of categories are related to sequence. Ideas may be classified according to simple to complex or categorized as a "first step" to the process being investigated. Sequencing of ideas is easily represented with animation. TealPaint 6.37 allows students to draw the ideas/concepts/subtopics in sequences and then animate the sequences to demonstrate the relationship.

ACTIVITY STRUCTURES RELATED TO INVESTIGATING, RESEARCHING, COLLECTING BACKGROUND INFORMATION

Data collection can be as simple as the act of reviewing information on the Internet and recording data in a database or word document for analysis at a later time. Using HHCs to digitally collect information means that data can be shared, updated, and manipulated easily.

Because reading activities are the flip-side of writing activities, gathering information has been a process of reviewing books, materials, and other print resources to identify relevant information. Many reference books have been converted to eBooks with a format appropriate for handhelds. Dictionary, thesaurus, atlas, and other reference eBooks are now available–not to mention the thousands of fiction and nonfiction books available for download to student handheld computers. With supplemental HHC expansion cards, teachers can create class libraries or other data from the Web for the students to share.

In addition, the introduction of the Internet puts the resources of millions of written records at the fingertips of every classroom teacher with Internet access. Several activity structures that use the Internet as a resource for data are supported by the use of HHCs in these data collection endeavors:

- *A virtual field trip* is a field trip that uses the Internet instead of a bus to transport students to an opportunity for real world learning. The teacher provides a study guide (usually in the form of a text document in Memos or QuickWord) that steps the students virtually through a selection of Internet Web sites. The study guide also includes instructions for activities students should complete, questions students should answer, or information students should collect at each of the Web sites. Teacher-created virtual field trips can be posted on the Internet with active links to other sites that students visit. AvantGo is a free online tool that accesses the online virtual field trip and related links, compresses the information, and provides it to the HHC during the synchronization process. Students have access to all of the information they would have had online, but in a portable format that can go home with them or to a field site without wireless access.

- *A linklist* is a list of Web site URLs that are activated so that the student can click on each link and access a Web page with relevant information. For example, the teacher can construct a list of Web sites that provide detailed information on several different insects that the teacher knows frequently visit the schoolyard. The students use the linklist as a "mini" field guide for identifying the insects. This activity may also be called a treasure hunt depending upon the instructional goals of the lesson. (See http://www.figg.com/handy4class/fieldguide.htm for an example of a field guide designed for download through AvantGo to student HHCs.)
- *A scavenger hunt,* a specialized linklist, is a set of questions that require students to use keywords to locate information to the questions. Beginning "surfers" are provided with keywords and links to appropriate search engines that will be successful in locating Web sites that contain the information to answer the questions. More advanced "surfers" may only be given appropriate search engines and be required to think of keywords on their own. (See http://www.figg.com/handy4class/hunt1.htm for an example of a scavenger hunt designed for download through AvantGo to student handhelds.)

HOW HANDHELDS SUPPORT ANALYZING DATA AND DRAWING CONCLUSIONS

Often, data analysis is a matter of reviewing the data collected and is dependent upon the quality and quantity of data available for review. Students who have used a database to record information are able to bring their data back into the classroom, and beam that record to a "master" database that collects all student data. The master database is then beamed back to the students for their work in analyzing the compiled data. Database tools for HHCs, such as HanDBase 3, incorporate graphic database forms that provide students with a guide for collecting the appropriate data needed for the analysis.

In addition to software applications, there are also peripherals that help students gather data and analyze it. Vernier and ImagiProbe make sensors that allow students to collect data regarding various indicators (e.g., temperature and acidity) in the field using the probe attached to the HHC. Data are then uploaded to a desktop computer with additional software that performs a number of different analyses as needed for different investigations.

- *Comparing data with digital collections:* Using HHCs, students create insect, flower, seed or tree collections by taking digital pictures of the subjects, which are then collected into a photo album with identifying information. In a similar manner, digital collections that document environmental resources are created by taking digital pictures of natural water sources in a certain habitat. Additional data are collected regarding the quality of these natural water sources using the Vernier or ImageProbe sensors that measure temperature and acidity of the water. The information can then be compared and analyzed in order to describe the environmental habitat being investigated. Thus, a digital collection is a compilation of related items in digital format. Each photo entry consists of a digital image and information that describes that particular sample. Students are then able to analyze or compare the digital images and related recorded notes to establish patterns or dissimilarities.

ACTIVITY STRUCTURES RELATED TO EVALUATION AND ASSESSMENT

Once students have collected data and made an analysis, sharing their findings with their classmates becomes an important evaluation activity. Or, perhaps at the end of the writing process, students publish their written piece. At this point, it is essential for the students to demonstrate the ability to synthesize their understandings into a presentation of some form.

There are several activity structures that can be used by students for this presentation purpose:

- *Characteristics books:* Identifying and classifying natural objects are two classification activities that often turn into occupations.

(For example, astronomers, biologists, physicists spend much of their time identifying and classifying natural phenomena.) The characteristics book/slideshow presents a characteristic of the object and invites the reader/viewer to identify the object from that characteristic. The next page/slide reveals the object being presented. Students can create the characteristic books in PowerPoint, which can be compressed using Presenter-To-Go desktop software and downloaded to the handheld. By connecting the Presenter-To-Go module to a LCD projector, the book can be viewed from the HHC.

- *Predictable books:* Maring, Boxie, and Wiseman (2000) define predictable books, or pattern books, as "texts for children that make use of repeated phrases and language patterns" and point to the importance of their use in teaching reading and writing because "children learn these patterns and then use prediction-confirmation strategies to 'read' the words in the story" (online). To extend the predictable books into the science classrooms, the books often depict patterns that are related to characteristics of animal, minerals, and plants to develop knowledge of those characteristics. Predictable books created using eBook Studio allow students to create the book and then "publish" the books in a downloadable form for HHCs. (See an example at http://www.figg.com/edt5555/predictables.htm.)
- *Photo sequences:* Taking multiple "fast-action" shots (taking a series of pictures one right after the other as quickly as the camera will take the pictures) captures the sequence of the investigation that allows examination of critical steps in the process. For example, to determine if the slope of an incline affects the speed that a marble rolls down the incline, marbles are rolled down inclines of the same length but set up at different slopes. The investigator would take "fast-action" shots to record the roll of the marbles down the inclines, and would be able to examine individual pictures to mark the movements of the marbles down the inclines for comparison purposes. The digital images can be uploaded to the computer and taken into a video editor such as iMovie or Premiere to create a small movie. The movie can be compressed (using software such as TealMovie) and downloaded to the HHC during the synchronization process. Students can take the movie with them as they conduct their own experiments or collect data.
- *Conceptual dictionary:* The conceptual dictionary presents a page or slide with the term to be defined and a definition of the idea or

concept. The next page/slide reveals an image that represents an example of the concept being defined. The conceptual dictionary can be constructed and presented using any of the methods above. Students can use the finished dictionary as "flash card" learning games for multiple subject areas. (See example online at http://www.figg.com/edt5555/conceptdictionary.htm.)

- *Rubric creation:* Students (or teachers) can construct rubric forms using database applications (such as HanDBase 3). The forms can be downloaded to the evaluator's handheld. When the teacher serves as evaluator, the teacher can grade the performance using the rubric and instantly beam the information to students. There are other examples of software made for assessment purposes that allow teachers to create assessment instruments. For instance, Quizzler is software that allows teachers to create assessment instruments that can be downloaded to student handhelds.

CONCLUDING COMMENTS

Computing power for everyone can become a reality in today's classrooms. It opens the door for a variety of teaching innovations to fit teaching styles for those with the initiative to walk through the door. Although we have provided examples of teaching with activity structures based on Palm OS software, activity structures work for any computer technology–HHCs make that technology mobile. With computing tools in the hands of all students, learning becomes portable and provides our students with life-long learning opportunities not possible with textbooks or traditional tools. The days of checking out the cart of laptops for a six-week project to complete the mandated technology requirement (that most curriculums include today) will be replaced by the delivery of instruction that seamlessly integrates technology a small piece at a time in every lesson–simply because the tools are portable, easy to use, encourage and support collaborative learning, and fit in the palm of your hand!

REFERENCES

Becker, H. J. (1994). How exemplary computer-using teachers differ from other teachers: Implications for realizing the potential of computers in schools. *Journal of Research on Computing in Education*, *26*(3), 291-321.

Becker, H. J., & Ravitz, J. L. (2001). *Computer use by teachers: Are Cuban's predictions correct?* Paper presented at the 2001 Annual Meeting of the American Educational Research Association, Seattle, WA.

CEO Forum on Education and Technology. (2001). *CEO Forum school technology and readiness report: Key building blocks for student achievement in the 21st century*. Retrieved October 17, 2004, from http://www.ceoforum.org/downloads/report4.pdf.

Hadley, M., & Sheingold, K. (1993, May). Commonalities and distinctive patterns of teachers' integration of computers. *American Journal of Education, 101*, 261-315.

Harris, J. B. (1998). *Virtual architecture: Designing and directing curriculum-based telecomputing*. Eugene, OR: International Society for Technology in Education.

Joyce, B. R., Weil, M., & Calhoun, E. (2003). *Models of teaching*. Boston: Allyn & Bacon.

Maring, G. H., Boxie, P., & Wiseman, B. J. (2000). School-university partnerships through online pattern books. *Reading Online*, *4*(5), Retrieved February 24, 2003, from http://www.readingonline.org/articles/art_index.asp?HREF=/articles/maring/index.html.

Park, J., & Staresina, L. N. (2004). *Tracking U.S. trends*. Retrieved October 17, 2004, from http://counts.edweek.org/sreports/tc04/article.cfm?slug=35tracking.h23.

Ringstaff, C., & Kelley, L. (2002). *The learning return on our educational technology investment*. Retrieved October 17, 2004, from http://www.wested.org/cs/we/view/rs/619.

Roblyer, M. D. (2003). *Integrating educational technology into teaching*. Columbus, OH: Merrill Prentice Hall.

Rozycki, W. (1999). *Just-in-time teaching*. Retrieved October 17, 2004, from http://www.indiana.edu/~rcapub/v22n1/p08.html.

SRI International. (2002). *Palm education pioneer's program: Final evaluation report*. Menlo Park, CA.

ANNOTATED LIST OF HARDWARE AND SOFTWARE APPLICATIONS CITED WITH CURRENT PRICING

DDH Software, Inc. HanDBase 3.012 ($29.95). Retrieved February 22, 2004, from http://www.ddhsoftware.com/handbase_palm.html?UID=2004022112455366.68.35.71. HanDBase is a mobile relational database with a very intuitive interface, many reliable yet powerful features, a new forms-designing capability, and an extensive collection of free databases to download and modify. Forms can be used to collect data from multiple users and then synchronize all the forms into one consolidated database.

iAnywhere Solutions, Inc. AvantGo. (Freeware). Retrieved February 24, 2004, from https://my.avantgo.com/home/. A free service that allows each user 2MB of Web space to hold predetermined Web pages or personalized lessons to be downloaded to a handheld computer.

Mobility Electronics, Inc. QuickWord 7.1 ($39.95). Retrieved February 24, 2004, from http://software.igo.com/basket.jsp?siteId=334&jid=49B9X2ADAAXC93A3X5152AFAA4CFCCFE. QuickWord, the word-processing facet of Quick Office 7.1, is built on the foundation of the industry-leading SmartDoc text editor/DOC reader, with seamless integration with Microsoft Word.

Inspiration for Palm OS ($29.95). Retrieved October 7, 2004, from http://www.inspiration.com/productinfo/inspirationpalmos/index.cfm. The learning benefits of Inspiration, the leading visual software, combine with the natural ease of handhelds to give students a tool for gathering information, developing ideas, capturing ideas, and showing relationships by sketching symbols and arranging thoughts directly on screen with a stylus. It's an innovative, versatile way to help students achieve clearer thinking, better writing, and improved performance across the curriculum.

MARGI Systems, Inc. Presenter-to-Go (SD Version $199.95), Retrieved February 23, 2004, from http://shop.store.yahoo.com/margistore/pressdcar.html. A complete presentation solution providing educators with a simple, fast, and flexible tool for the delivery of high-quality color presentations using the handheld device. The Mirror feature allows any file on the handheld device to be viewed with a projector or TV screen. Presenter-to-Go is now available for Palm SD card, making it adaptable for collaborative presentations.

Palm Digital Media (a division of PalmGear). Palm eBook Studio ($29.95). Retrieved February 23, 2004, from http://www.palmdigitalmedia.com/products/ebookstudio. Computer software, both Mac and Windows, that easily allows the design of navigation for a document, formats it, and converts the finished document for reading on a handheld.

Pocket Mobility, Inc. Quizzler (Freeware) and Quizzler Maker ($24.95). Retrieved February 24, 2004, from http://www.pocketmobility.com/quizzler/. The free version allows you to take true/false, multiple choice, picture identification, etc.,quizzes on the handheld created by Quizzler Maker, a Windows program that provides a simple user interface for creating quizzes.

TealPoint™. TealMovie 3.81 ($29.95). Retrieved February 23, 2004, from http://www.tealpoint.com/softmovi.htm. A handheld multimedia system that can turn any PalmOS handheld into a player of high-quality video and animation. This software offers smooth playback up to 60 frames per second, high-quality full screen TrueColor or grayscale imagery, plus a Windows converter program that easily creates compact TealMovie-format files from standard AVI, Quicktime, and WAV files.

TealPoint™. Teal Paint™ 6.37 ($19.95). Retrieved February 22, 2004, from http://www.tealpoint.com/softpnt.htm. A paint and sketch program for Palm OS that supports a slideshow mode, programmable buttons, image compression, grid snap, image templates, copy/paste and screen-grabbing. It allows hi-resolution graphics, 16-bit color and grayscale support, unlimited image size, six zoom levels, animation, and multiple level undo, plus the 20 drawing tools, 16 patterns, 24 brushes and layers. There are also extensive freeware support files of clip art and backgrounds.

HARDWARE

Zire 72 Handheld Computer (~$250)–http://www.palmone.com/us/support/zire72/.

Venier Sensors (Prices vary from $21 to $239 for different probes)–http://www.vernier.com/.

ImagiProbe Sensors (Interface plus three sensors $249)–http://www.imagiworks.com/Pages/Products/ImagiProbe.html

.

Foo Seau Yoon
Jeanne Ho
John G. Hedberg

Teachers as Designers of Learning Environments

SUMMARY. This study examined how six Singapore teachers approached the design and implementation of a unit of work (topic) to demonstrate exemplary classroom practices that engage learners and use ICT in knowledge-generative rather than presentational activities. After a reflection and feedback session on the first lesson observation involving the researcher and the teacher, the teacher redesigned the lesson to enhance ICT use and involve students more actively in their learning. Our study revealed that there is a difference between students' physical

FOO SEAU YOON is an Educational Technology Officer, Research & Development Section, Educational Technology Division, Ministry of Education, Singapore 138675 (E-mail: FOO_Seau_Yoon@moe.gov.sg).
JEANNE HO is Senior Head, Research & Development Section, Educational Technology Division, Ministry of Education, Singapore 138675 (E-mail: Jeanne_Marie_HO@moe.gov.sg).
JOHN G. HEDBERG is Professor, Learning Sciences and Technology, National Institute of Education, Nanyang Technological University, Singapore 637616 (E-mail: jhedberg@nie.edu.sg).
The authors wish to acknowledge the contributions of the following Ministry of Education officers who worked with the six teachers in this research study: Aw Wai Lin, Azizah Rabunam, Ban Pei Ling, Fauziah Adiman, Lim-Lee Li Li, Leow Li Quin, Lynde Tan, Nora Crothers, and S. Ravindran.

[Haworth co-indexing entry note]: "Teachers as Designers of Learning Environments." Yoon, Foo Seau, Jeanne Ho, and John G. Hedberg. Co-published simultaneously in *Computers in the Schools* (The Haworth Press, Inc.) Vol. 22, No. 3/4, 2005, pp. 145-157; and: *Classroom Integration of Type II Uses of Technology in Education* (ed: Cleborne D. Maddux, and D. LaMont Johnson) The Haworth Press, Inc., 2005, pp. 145-157. Single or multiple copies of this article are available for a fee from The Haworth Document Delivery Service [1-800-HAWORTH, 9:00 a.m. - 5:00 p.m. (EST). E-mail address: docdelivery@haworthpress.com].

Available online at http://www.haworthpress.com/web/CITS

doi:10.1300/J025v22n03_12

engagement and cognitive engagement in a task and that the teacher, as a designer of the learning environment, needs to make explicit the cognitive processes involved in using the tool to ensure students' effective use of ICT. The teachers' understanding of what constitutes effective learning and their roles in students' learning determine how they design the learning environment. In essence, it is the teacher's skill in managing the "tripartite" partnership of IT tool, learning task, and teacher support that brings about higher levels of student engagement.

KEYWORDS. Student engagement, teacher support, learning task, teachers as designers of learning environments, effective use of ICT

TEACHERS AS TASK DESIGNERS

Hawkins (1996), writing in the middle of a long-term project concerned with the use of technology to enhance teaching and learning in North American schools, commented that:

> Beyond the tradition of instructing the fixed facts of disciplines and received knowledge, schools must now enable students to appreciate the complexities that bathe them–to develop sophisticated interpretation skills, tolerance for ambiguity, an appetite for difficult problems, and measured thoughtfulness in pursuit of solution. This requires creating habits of seeking out various perspectives and consulting multiple disciplines and any big question. It requires facility with tools that help us find and make sense of evidence. It requires openness to conversation as a way to challenge one's assumptions, and a habit of remaining interested in ways of conceiving things. (p. 40)

Hawkins' comments provide the basis for investigating how teachers function as learning activity designers. Three critical factors need to be considered and manipulated if one is to move toward more open-textured learning activity designs and use ICT tools efficiently and effectively at the same time. Simply put, in whatever is produced or implemented, scope needs to be provided for multiple solutions (end points may be validly different), multiple strategies (the route to an end point is often generated by the invention of the learner and the needs of the data being generated as part of the process), and multiple perspectives (the perspective of the problem might be instrumental in a solution or an alternative approach given a different point of view).

In the United States, when teachers were involved in the ACOT (Apple Classrooms of Tomorrow) project from 1985-1998, they were observed to pass through five phases of development as their traditional beliefs about education and classroom practices were gradually replaced with new ones as a result of being situated in technology-rich learning environments. Summarizing Sandholtz, Ringstaff, and Dwyer (1997), teachers at the *Entry* level frequently found that they were unable to anticipate problems in their classrooms. At the *Adoption* level, teachers delivered teacher-centered lessons but also began to anticipate problems and develop strategies for solving them. At the level of *Adaptation*, teachers started using technology to their advantage and began to embrace student-centered orientations. At the level of *Appropriation*, teachers' personal attitudes to technology changed to confident expert and willing learner; and finally with *Invention*, teachers were disposed to view learning as an active, creative, and social process.

Following the ACOT model provides a framework for coming to terms with learning activity design issues by positing that teachers, as task-designers, could be potentially involved in increasing the effectiveness of their use of ICT as they understand more about the technologies and how they support different learning strategies. This study sought to work with classroom teachers who were nominated as being at higher levels of technology implementation and who took up the challenge of supporting effective learning with high levels of student participation.

STUDENT ENGAGEMENT

Recent literature (Chapman, 2003) points to using a combination of cognitive (e.g., students expending mental efforts to learn something), behavioral (e.g., students' participation), and affective criteria (e.g., students' enthusiasm and interest) to assess student engagement. More specifically, Jones, Valdez, Nowakowski, and Rasmussen (1995) presented a comprehensive framework for the concept of engaged learning within the context of ICT use. It comprises 26 indicators for engaged learning that are organized into eight categories of learning and instruction (e.g., vision of learning, teacher role). Jones' et al. eight categories of learning and instruction were used to code the teachers' ICT-based lessons and interview data in our study.

EFFECTIVE USE OF ICT

Researchers such as Jones et al. (1995), Roschelle, Pea, Hoadley, Gordin and Means (2000), Bransford, Brown, and Cocking (1999), Jonassen (2000), and Maddux, Johnson, and Willis (2001) indicated that students learn best when they are actively constructing new knowledge rather than passively acquiring knowledge. From Jonassen's mindtools (e.g., semantic organization tools, semantic networking tools) to Maddux's Type II technology applications (e.g., applications that place the control on the learners to involve them actively and intellectually), it can be seen that the role of technology is to effectively support the processes of student knowledge construction. On the basis of the literature, a checklist was derived to identify the "Value-Add" of ICT in the lessons that the teachers submitted for our study.

METHODOLOGY

Case Study Approach

According to Yin (1994), the case study approach is ideal for holistic in-depth investigation of a phenomenon in its real-life context. The case study method was used to obtain rich descriptions of the pedagogical practices of teachers whose lessons support ICT use and engaged learning. Teachers, who were invited to submit lesson proposals for the study, were recommended by our colleagues who had been working closely with schools or they were identified from past winners of innovative uses of technology awards. Six proposals, covering a range of subjects, levels, and use of technology, were shortlisted from a total of 17 submitted proposals. Lessons chosen were conducted during curriculum time and appeared to be well structured in terms of learning tasks. In addition, technology played a central role to engage the learners and was employed generatively to support knowledge building.

Data Collection

Data collection took place over a five-week period, with the researchers working in pairs on each case. A pre-lesson interview determined the teacher's views and beliefs about the role of ICT in learning. This was followed by a lesson observation to see how the teacher's intent, as indicated in the lesson plan and pre-lesson interview, was translated into classroom processes and practices. The researchers took extensive notes of teacher actions and class talk, and observed selected student groups working on a learning task. A post-lesson interview was conducted with the teachers to review the lesson and surface possible gaps between the teacher's beliefs, practices, and outcomes. Jones' et al. (1995) framework of engaged learning indicators was introduced to the teacher with the aim of helping the teacher identify ideas for redesigning the lesson to shift it more toward one that might be described as active, engaging, and generative for the students. The teacher was given time to redesign his or her lesson ideas and to conduct either a follow-up lesson with the same class or the redesigned lesson with another class of similar ability. The second lesson was videotaped in its entirety and a second post-lesson interview was conducted to explore the teacher's new insights and understanding of the role of ICT in the learning experience.

Data Coding and Analysis

The lessons were coded using Jones' et al. (1995) eight categories of learning and instruction. An additional category of the "Value Add of ICT" was added to each case description to focus the analysis on the role of ICT. Notes were also made on obstacles/problems encountered and the teacher's perceptions of what constitutes effective learning. Each case study was reviewed by the whole research team to ensure that the description and analysis of each case would be comprehensive and triangulated. The description was kept factual while the analysis was based on what was said or observed during the lessons and on the teacher's views and opinions as expressed during the interviews.

DISCUSSION

We propose using a tripartite model (see Figure 1) to anchor the discussion of our findings. The tripartite model describes the interplay of

FIGURE 1. Tripartite model adapted from Oliver's (1999) learning design construct.

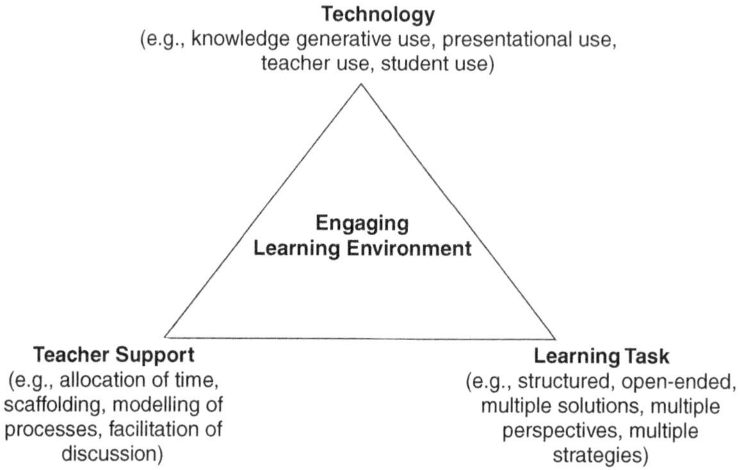

technology, learning task, and teacher support that determines whether learning experiences are engaging to students.

The proposed tripartite model is adapted from Oliver's (1999) learning design construct. According to Oliver, each ICT-mediated learning design comprises three key elements, that of tasks that the learners are required to do, resources that support learners to conduct the task, and support mechanisms provided by the teacher.

We noted a difference between students' physical engagement and cognitive engagement in a task and that the teacher, as a designer of the learning environment, needs to make explicit the cognitive processes involved in using the tool to ensure students' effective use of ICT.

In Denise's first geography lesson, students had to use the Inspiration software (a software for mindmapping) to note useful and relevant information when listening to the group presentations on environmental issues. For the duration of the learning task, students were physically engaged in creating text bubbles, drawing arrows, and switching colors on their screens. Although most students were technically competent in using Inspiration, they did not fully categorize their points nor link them coherently.

When designing the learning task for her first lesson, Denise had assumed that her students would know how to use the features provided by Inspiration to support their mental process of organizing information. In the follow-up lesson, Denise decided to make explicit the cognitive processes involved in organizing and categorizing information. Table 1 shows how Denise provided additional teacher support for the learning task in her redesigned lesson.

During her redesigned lesson, Denise modelled how to categorize and link information. She asked students key questions such as "How is information chunked?" and gave them specific pointers using one student's work:

> Is there anything wrong with this schema or is there anything you think doesn't quite fit? . . . It lacks differentiation between what is the statement of the concept, what is the explanation of the concept and what is actually an example. . . . (Lesson Observation Notes)

Also, she gave an example of the kind of mindmaps that students were expected to produce:

> Notice that under desertification, there may be 2 major concepts of what the effects are and then the possible solutions to the effects. . . .

TABLE 1. Tripartite Elements for Denise's Learning Task Using Inspiration

Learning Task	**Technology**	**Teacher Support**
Students took notes of the main points provided by two group presentations.	Inspiration software	First Lesson *Lack of teacher support* Denise gave general instructions on how to use the software and some possible categories for organizing the information.
		Redesigned Lesson *Additional teacher support provided* Denise modelled the cognitive processes involved in organizing the information, allocated more time to the task, and asked presenters to circulate among the groups.

So this is an example of a chunked thing that I would expect from you at the end of the time. . . . (Lesson Observation Notes)

In addition, Denise allocated additional time for students to do the Inspiration task. She also instructed the presenters to circulate among their classmates to "help the rest with the chunking and grouping of the information" (Lesson Observation Notes). As a result, there was more cognitive engagement on the part of the students as they focused more on linking the different categories as compared to the first lesson. The digital mindmaps they produced were more coherently organized.

We observed that the lessons in our study revealed a continuum of ICT use. How ICT is used depends on the teachers' understanding of what constitutes effective learning and their roles in students' learning.

Andrew is one example of a teacher whose use of ICT reflected his understanding of what constitutes effective learning and his role in his students' learning. According to Andrew, an effective learning environment is one that is sufficiently open to encourage multiple perspectives and collaboration and it places the onus on the students to make sense of their own learning. He felt that his role as a teacher is to facilitate students' learning: "I don't know if you noticed my style; I tend to like to ask questions more than to give answers and I like to ask as many questions as time permits" (Post-Lesson Interview).

His understanding of what effective learning entails and his role in the learning process influenced the way he designed his English lessons. Andrew wanted his students to incorporate the main components of a story (e.g., character, climax) in their writing of a short narrative. He deliberately chose open-ended IT resources (digital movie trailer, still images, and Microsoft Word), designed a learning task that afforded multiple perspectives and solutions (students could choose to replicate a movie plot or create a new one), and used open-ended questions to guide student discussions (see Table 2).

Andrew used the movie trailer because it was sufficiently ambiguous to support different interpretations. He also provided a large range of digital pictures that gave different perspectives of the same scenes to generate discussions, develop multiple perspectives and spark creativity:

I would try to take pictures that were quite similar . . . and since there were quite a few scenes where the spikes flew out and different angles of the ball rolling, I had to put in more so that it would

TABLE 2. Tripartite Elements for Andrew's Learning Task

Learning Task	Technology	Teacher Support
Students worked in groups to incorporate the elements of a story (e.g., setting, climax, problem) in their writing of a short narrative.	Digital movie clip, digital still images, and Microsoft Word	Open-ended questioning to probe students' understanding.

> [allow] for flexibility of interpretation. Had I given fewer pictures and tell-tale pictures, then it would have been too predictive and everybody would naturally be locked into thinking what had happened, what did not happen. (Post-Lesson Interview)

In Andrew's English lessons, pairs of students within each group viewed separately a movie trailer and a set of digital images. To get the full picture, the two pairs within each group came together to co-construct the story by pooling their knowledge and experiences.

Andrew left it open to students to negotiate whether to replicate the original plot or create a new plot:

> This class is a mixed ability class so there is virtually no way to allow the creativity and yet insist that they recreate. . . . If I insisted that they recreate, that would also hamper their creativity and then they would be forced to think of alternative forms. (Post-Lesson Interview)

Collaboratively shaping their story using Microsoft Word supported students' continual improvisation of their story (e.g., editing features like undelete and spellcheck) and provided a platform for students to make their thinking visible. Students used different colors (e.g., green for setting and character, dark blue for rising action, red for climax, plum for resolution, orange for coda) to indicate the story components within their story. This provided feedback to both the students and the teacher on how well they had understood the different story components:

> There was one child who selected all red (indicating climax), so I asked and said, "Are you sure that everything is red; is that it?" and I pointed out certain phrases, and he was then able to realize that it shouldn't have been all red, and then he himself uncolored that particular portion. (Post-Lesson Interview)

In presenting their stories for class review or critique, the groups had to explain how they crafted their stories. Learning was made public so that each group could get input from other groups (i.e., diverse perspectives) and build on their knowledge (i.e., improve their story). Andrew facilitated students' learning by asking mainly open-ended questions, and giving them the opportunity to explain their multiple solutions (different stories).

Student 3: We started with dialogue which makes it sound better.
Andrew: Why do you say it sounds better?
Student 1: Because normally stories start without dialogue, they just start off. We wanted it to sound more interesting, more unique so we had a dialogue.
Andrew: How does that contribute to character development?
Student 4: It shows what the character is feeling.
Student 3: His emotions.
Student 1: It gives the reader a headstart on what the character is like. (Lesson 2 Observation Notes)

> *We observed that it is the teacher's skill in managing the "tripartite" partnership of IT tool (to be chosen with careful thought and with appropriateness), learning task (to design with the students' ability in mind) and teacher support (provision of adequate support in terms of modelling/scaffolding of key processes and allocation of sufficient time) that brings about higher levels of student engagement.*

One of Denise's learning tasks was to get students to ask questions online to consolidate their understanding of environmental issues. For this task, she managed very successfully the tripartite partnership of IT tool (discussion forum), learning task (students asking higher order questions) and teacher support (modelling the process of asking questions) to bring about high levels of student engagement (see Table 3).

Denise noticed that the initial student exchanges in the discussion forum were relatively low level and consisted mainly of standard definition-related questions such as "What is informal settlement? Please define . . ." and "What is urban decay?" Denise went into the discussion forum to model the process of asking higher order questions: "Air pollution people: How are you going to 'implement laws'? Have you considered the political implications of such a move?" (Discussion Forum).

TABLE 3. Tripartite Elements for Denise's Learning Task Involving a Discussion Forum

Learning Task	Technology	Teacher Support
Students were to ask higher order questions regarding the presentations.	Online discussion forum	Denise modelled the process of asking higher order questions and of providing comprehensive answers.

It was observed that the students took their cue from their teacher's demonstration of the kind of thinking she expected from them and subsequently, the kinds of students' questions and comments posted improved and there were more higher order questions: "How do you allocate the funds in each aspect? What laws do you want to implement? Where do you want to start from and where?" (Discussion Forum).

In the words of Denise (post-lesson interview), the discussion forum had helped her students make public their learning so that others can actually get that knowledge but also open it up for discussion. An example of how student presenters defended the solutions they had proposed is shown in Figure 2.

Discussions and student collaboration went beyond the lesson when some students returned to the forum later in the day to post more questions or comments. Denise indicated that in a normal class setting, students who processed their thoughts more slowly would be left out of the discussion. Denise commented:

> In classroom situations, you ask them to ask questions, [the] tendency is [they think that the] teacher is king, so they won't ask. They won't ask unless they are really sure of themselves . . . they will just listen. But in front of a computer, they respond and they are engaged in that. (Pre-Lesson Interview)

CONCLUDING REMARKS

From the discussion of the case studies, it is clear that the capability of the technology itself will not ensure that there is higher student involvement in learning. It is the teacher's skill in managing the tripartite partnership of IT tool, learning task, and teacher support that brings about higher levels of student engagement. Our study revealed that there is a difference between students' physical engagement and cogni-

FIGURE 2. Students defending their proposed solution in the discussion forum.

Gohyee3aw
Level: Jr. Member
Posts: 13
IP: Logged

Re: Re: Geography ~ Environmental Degradation

denisec.wdl wrote:
Desertifiers* ~ a lot of the solutions need to be carried out by the government . . . . how are you going to get their cooperation, considering the politics involved?
(*Desertifiers comprised the groups of pupils who were looking into solutions to reduce the process of desertification whereby formerly productive land degraded.)

one avenue could be international pressure on those countries, spearheaded especially by the UN, known for its stand on Human Rights. Highlight the potential problems, both economic and social, that the government may face if the problem is not solved

- EThan AND kALPANA

08-07-2003 at 12:33 AM Quote Reply

tive engagement in a task and that the teacher, as a designer of the learning environment, needs to make explicit the cognitive processes involved in using the tool to ensure students' effective use of ICT. In addition, the teachers' understanding of what constitutes effective learning and their roles in students' learning determine how they design the learning environment. The tripartite model could serve as a frame of reference for teachers to discuss, understand, and analyze the dynamics involved in implementing ICT-based lessons.

REFERENCES

Bransford, J. D., Brown, A. L., Cocking, R. R. (Eds). (1999). *How people learn: Brain, mind, experience, and School* [Electronic Version]. Washington, DC: National Academy Press.

Chapman, E. (2003). Alternative approaches to assessing student engagement rates. *Practical Assessment, Research & Evaluation, 8(13).* Retrieved November 18, 2003, from http://PAREonline.net/getvn.asp?v=8&n=13

Hawkins, J. (1996). Dilemmas. In C. Fisher, D. C. Dwyer, & K. Yocam (Eds.), *Education and technology: Reflections on computing in classrooms* (pp. 35-50). San Francisco: Jossey-Bass.

Jonassen, D. H. (2000). *Computers as mindtools for schools: Engaging critical thinking* (2nd ed). Upple Saddle River, NJ: Merrill/Prentice Hall.

Jones, B. F., Valdez, G., Nowakowski, J., & Rasmussen, C. (1995). *Plugging in: Choosing and using technology.* North Central Regional Educational Laboratory. Retrieved March 7, 2003, from http://www.ncrel.org/sdrs/edtalk/toc.htm

Maddux, C. D., Johnson, D. L., & Willis, J. W. (2001). *Educational computing: Learning with tomorrow's technologies* (3rd ed). Boston: Allyn & Bacon.

Oliver, R. (1999). Exploring strategies for online teaching and learning. *Distance Education, 20*(2), 240-254.

Roschelle, J. M., Pea, R. D., Hoadley, C. M., Gordin, D. N., & Means, B. M. (2000). Changing how and what children learn in school with computer-based technologies [Electronic Version]. *Children and Computer Technology, 10*(2), 76-101.

Sandholtz, J. H., Ringstaff, C., & Dwyer D. C. (Eds.). (1997). *Teaching with technology: Creating student-centered classrooms.* New York: Teachers College Press.

Yin, R. K. (1994). *Case study research: Design and methods* (2nd ed). Thousand Oaks, CA: Sage.

Min Liu

The Effect of a Hypermedia Learning Environment on Middle School Students' Motivation, Attitude, and Science Knowledge

SUMMARY. This study examined the effect of a hypermedia-enhanced problem-based learning environment in astronomy on sixth-graders' science knowledge, attitude toward learning science, and motivation toward learning. It was found that the students had significantly increased their science knowledge from pretest to posttest and also retained much of what they had learned after two weeks. Students' attitudes toward science and their intrinsic goal orientation were significantly higher after using the technology application. Students' science knowledge scores were positively related to their attitudes and intrinsic goal orientation. Such findings suggested that this hypermedia learning environment had a positive impact on the sixth-graders. *[Article copies available for a fee from The Haworth Document Delivery Service: 1-800-HAWORTH. E-mail address: <docdelivery@haworthpress.com> Website: <http://www.HaworthPress.com> © 2005 by The Haworth Press, Inc. All rights reserved.]*

MIN LIU is Associate Professor, IT Program Area Coordinator, and Graduate Advisor, Instructional Technology Program, Department of Curriculum and Instruction, The University of Texas at Austin, Austin, TX 78712-0379 (E-mail: MLiu@mail.utexas.edu).

[Haworth co-indexing entry note]: "The Effect of a Hypermedia Learning Environment on Middle School Students' Motivation, Attitude, and Science Knowledge." Liu, Min. Co-published simultaneously in *Computers in the Schools* (The Haworth Press, Inc.) Vol. 22, No. 3/4, 2005, pp. 159-171; and: *Classroom Integration of Type II Uses of Technology in Education* (ed: Cleborne D. Maddux, and D. LaMont Johnson) The Haworth Press, Inc., 2005, pp. 159-171. Single or multiple copies of this article are available for a fee from The Haworth Document Delivery Service [1-800-HAWORTH, 9:00 a.m. - 5:00 p.m. (EST). E-mail address: docdelivery@haworthpress.com].

Available online at http://www.haworthpress.com/web/CITS

doi:10.1300/J025v22n03_13

KEYWORDS. Problem-based learning, technology, attitude, motivation, science, hypermedia

RESEARCH FRAMEWORK

Problem-based learning (PBL) exemplifies student-centered learning and emphasizes solving complex problems in rich contexts. PBL has been shown to result in better long-term content retention than traditional instruction, and supports the development of problem-solving skills (Hmelo & Ferrari, 1997; Norman & Schmidt, 1992).

Implementing PBL in classrooms without technology proves to be challenging. Its implementation challenges include ineffective ways to present the central problem through oral or written means, large investment in time and effort to develop PBL units, initial discomfort with the methodology from the learners and instructors, and the need for new forms of assessment (Hoffman & Richie, 1997). The constraints in a K-12 setting such as large class sizes, short class periods, and full and fixed schedules by teachers and students make it especially difficult to use PBL in a K-12 classroom.

Technology has been suggested as a way to address some of these challenges. Hoffman and Richie (1997) recommended the use of hypermedia to deliver problem scenarios to help "students comprehend the situation and see the relevance of various contextual elements" (p. 102). The nonlinear, associative, and interactive capabilities of hypermedia can allow students to access information according to their own learning needs and provide rich information resources through different media in a more efficient way (Hoffman & Richie, 1997). Hypermedia-enhanced PBL can engage students in cognitive activities that would be out of their reach otherwise, and assist learners to generate and test hypotheses through simulations. When hypermedia-based tools are used to enhance the cognitive powers of learners during their thinking, problem-solving, and learning, they become cognitive tools (Jonassen & Reeves, 1996). Cognitive tools can enhance PBL delivery and provide necessary support to learners. In this study, we examined the impact of a hypermedia-enhanced PBL application on sixth-graders' learning. We also looked at factors that are of importance to learning such as motivation, attitudes, and gender.

Motivation

Literature on motivation and classroom learning has shown that motivation plays an important role in influencing learning and achievement (Ames, 1990). If motivated, students tend to approach challenging tasks eagerly, persist in difficulty, and take pleasure in their achievement (Stipek, 1993). Research has also shown that instructional context strongly affects students' motivation. Instructional materials that are challenging, give students choices, and promote perceived autonomy and self-determination can have a positive effect on students' motivation (Hidi & Harackiewicz, 2000).

Attitude

Students with positive attitudes are more likely to sustain their efforts and have the desire to be involved in the learning tasks. There is some evidence that attitude toward science relates positively with achievement (Mattern & Schau, 2002). In reviewing the literature about attitudes toward science over the past 20 years, Osborne, Simon, and Collins (2003) noted that research indicated a decline in attitudes toward science from age 11 onward and an apparent contradiction between students' attitudes toward science in general and their attitudes toward school science. In reviewing factors that can influence attitudes, Osborne et al. emphasized that how science materials are taught in classrooms can affect students' attitudes.

Gender

The concern over the shortage of highly qualified scientists, especially female scientists, has highlighted the need of science education for all students (Jarvis & Pell, 2002). The belief is that if students develop positive attitudes toward science and enjoy learning science during their middle school years, they will be more likely to pursue a career in science later on. Research on gender and attitudes toward science, however, is mixed. Some studies have shown girls' attitudes toward science are significantly less positive than boys (Hendley, Stables, & Stables, 1996). Other studies have indicated that girls are confident of their ability to take science classes and are doing as well as boys in the traditionally "masculine" subjects (Whitehead, 1996). The inconclusive finding on gender, attitude, and learning is an indication that more research is needed.

PURPOSE OF THE STUDY AND RESEARCH QUESTIONS

The purpose of this study was to examine the effectiveness of a hypermedia PBL application built for sixth-graders. A previous study investigated how students with different ability levels performed in this hypermedia environment (Liu, 2004). This study replicates the previous research by increasing the sample size from one middle school to four middle schools. In addition to examining any change in students' attitudes and science knowledge from pretest to posttest, this study extends the previous one by looking at students' retention of science knowledge and their motivation. Three research questions guided this study:

1. What is the effect of the hypermedia PBL environment on sixth-graders' acquisition and retention of science knowledge? Are there any differences in science knowledge between male and female students after using the program?
2. What is the effect of the hypermedia PBL environment on sixth-graders' motivation toward learning and attitude toward science? Are there any differences in attitude and motivation between male and female students after using the program?
3. Is there a relationship between students' attitudes toward science learning, motivation, and science knowledge?

METHOD

A Hypermedia Application

The hypermedia PBL application used in the study was Alien Rescue (more information can be found at http://jabba.edb.utexas.edu/alienrescue/). Alien Rescue engages sixth-grade students in solving a complex problem that requires them to gain specific knowledge about both our solar system and the tools and procedures scientists use to study it (Liu, Williams, & Pedersen, 2002). The program begins with a multimedia presentation of an ill-structured problem for students to solve. A group of six species of aliens, different in their characteristics, have arrived in Earth orbit, due to the destruction of their home planets. They must find new homes that can support their life forms or they will die. Students, acting as scientists, are asked to participate in this rescue operation, and their task is to determine the most suitable relocation site for each alien species. To solve this problem, students must engage in a variety of problem-solving activities. They need to research the aliens' needs, what the planets in our solar system can offer, and find possible matches. Students must sift through the vast information to decide what is relevant and important, and engage in planning and decision making as they determine how to use the resources of the solar system effectively.

To assist students in their problem solving, a set of cognitive tools performing various functions is provided. These tools are designed to share cognitive load, support cognitive processes, support cognitive activities that would be out of reach otherwise, and allow hypotheses generation and testing (Lajoie, 1993). For example, the four databases in Alien Rescue are carefully constructed and well-organized knowledge databases enhanced with graphics, animations, and 3-D videos. If students want to search for what a species looks like, where they live, the atmosphere and gravity on a planet, or past NASA missions, they can access such information readily in the *alien database*, *solar database*, and *mission database*. If they come across a scientific concept with which they are unfamiliar, they can look it up in the *concept database* that provides visually illustrated tutorials on various science topics. Such tools help reduce the memory burden for the students and put the multimedia-enriched information at students' fingertips.

Participants and Setting

Four hundred thirty-seven sixth-graders from four middle schools in a mid-sized southwestern city participated in the study. All participants were from regular education classes and 50% of them ($n = 222$) were female students. Four teachers taught these 22 science classes.

Students used Alien Rescue in their daily 45-minute science class for 15 days in the later part of the school year. The science teachers used Alien Rescue in place of the regular teaching materials on the solar system unit. Students worked in the computer labs and had access to computers for their own use. Students were assigned to groups of two or three by the teachers to solve the central problem collaboratively. In day one, after watching the video scenario, the teachers and the students held a discussion about their primary task. For the rest of the 15 days, teachers allowed the students to decide what their learning tasks were for each day and how to approach the problem. Although each teacher had his/her own ways of facilitation, classroom observations showed that each day the teachers began the lesson with a mini-discussion on what the students did on the previous day and addressed questions that came up. Students' questions were often answered by more questions from the teachers or answered by other students. Then, the students worked on the computer. The teachers answered students' questions, checked their progress, and ensured students were on task. Most days, the lesson ended with another short discussion about what the students accomplished that day, any questions that surfaced, and what the learning goal should be for the next day. Because all the necessary tools for students to work on the problem were provided via technology in this hypermedia environment, it was possible for the teachers to spend most of their class time interacting with the students individually. The teachers facilitated their students' learning through daily questioning, answering, and discussion.

Instrumentation and Analyses

Science knowledge test. Students' understanding of the science concepts introduced in Alien Rescue was measured by a 25-item multiple-choice test with a KR(20) of .73. Since no direct teaching was noted in using Alien Rescue (see the previous section), a good score on the test would indicate the student has acquired a good understanding of the scientific topics through his or her self-directed learning, classroom discussions, and/or peer interaction. This test was given both prior to and after using Alien Rescue. The test was also given to the students from one school two weeks after the completion of Alien Rescue to measure their retention of the knowledge. Because the other three schools used the program close to the end of the school year, there was insufficient time to administer the test again before the school year ended. Given that there were at least 15 days between the pretest and posttest, the pretest should not have served as a cue to the students. Students were not told about the retention test.

Motivation questionnaire. Eight items from the *Motivated Strategies for Learning Questionnaire* (MSLQ, Pintrich, Smith, Garcia, & McKeachie, 1991) were used to assess students' intrinsic goal orientation (4 items with a reported reliability coefficient of .74) and extrinsic goal orientation (4 items with a reported reliability coefficient of .62). Sample statements are "In a class like this, I prefer course material that really challenges me so I can learn new things," and "Getting a good grade in this class is the most rewarding thing for me right now." A seven-point Likert-type scale was used, with 1 being "not at all true of me" and 7 being "very true of me." This instrument was given before and after the use of Alien Rescue. In completing the post-survey, students were told that "this class" in each statement was defined as science classes taught like Alien Rescue.

Attitude toward science questionnaire. Students' attitudes toward science was measured using the *Attitude Toward Science in School Assessment* (ATSSA, Germann, 1988), which has a reported Cronbach's alpha of 0.95. The instrument consists of 14 Likert-scale items, with 1 being "strongly disagree" and 5 being "strongly agree." Sample statements include "Science is fun," and "During science classes, I usually am interested." The instrument was given before and after the use of Alien Rescue. In completing the post-survey, students were told that "science" in each statement was defined as science classes taught like Alien Rescue.

Four two-factor, 2 × 2, mixed ANOVAs were performed with gender as a between-subjects independent variable and time of testing (pretest, posttest) as the repeated measure within-subject variable. Students' science knowledge test scores, and scores for intrinsic goal orientation, extrinsic goal orientation, and attitudes toward science served as dependent variables respectively for each analysis. For retention on science knowledge, a two-factor, 2 × 3, mixed ANOVA was run with gender as a between-subjects independent variable and time of testing (pretest, posttest, retention) as the repeated measure within-subject variable. The dependent variable was students' science knowledge test scores. A correlation analysis was performed with post-scores of intrinsic goal orientation, extrinsic goal orientation, attitudes, and the science knowledge test.

Interviews. Toward the end of the study, interviews were conducted with 30% of the students, randomly selected, from each of the 22 classes. The interviews focused on what the students learned from using Alien Rescue, and why they liked or disliked Alien Rescue. The interview data were transcribed, then coded and categorized following the guidelines by Miles and Huberman (1994). Patterns from the data were extracted. The data were sorted into categories and subcategories according to their common themes and shared relationships. The qualitative data were used to substantiate the results from the statistical analyses.

RESULTS

Science Knowledge

The 2 × 2 mixed ANOVA indicated that there was not a significant two-way interaction between gender and time of testing (pretest, posttest) for the science knowledge tests: $F(1,415) = 3.94$, $p = .06$ (n = 417). Although there was not a main effect for gender, there was a main effect for the time of testing. The posttest scores for both male and female students were significantly higher than their pretest scores: $F(1,415) = 545.99$, $p < .01$ (see Table 1). The results of the 2 × 3, mixed ANOVA showed that there was not a significant two-way interaction between the gender and time of testing (pretest, posttest, retention): $F(2,196) = 2.65$, $p = .07$ (n = 100) (see Table 1). However, there was a main effect for the time of testing. For both male and female students, their posttest scores were significantly higher than their pretest scores–($t(99) = -11.62$, $p < .01$)–and their retention scores–($t(99) = 6.98$, $p <$ .01. Their retention scores were significantly higher than their pretest scores–$t(99) = -7.62$, $p < .01$–but lower than their posttest scores.

Motivation and Attitude

Motivation. The results of the 2 × 2 mixed ANOVAs indicated that there were no significant two-way interactions between gender and time of testing (pretest, posttest) for intrinsic goal orientation and extrinsic goal orientation: $F(1, 418)_{intrinsic} = .20$, $p = .65$, $n = 420$; $F(1,420)_{extrinsic}$ = .10, $p = .75$, $n = 422$ (see Table 2). However, there was a significant main effect for time of testing for intrinsic goal orientation: $F(1, 418)_{intrinsic}$ =

TABLE 1. Means and Standard Deviations (in Parenthesis) for the Science Knowledge Test

Gender	*n*	Science Knowledge Test (score from 0-100)		
		Pre-	Post-	Retention-
Male	205	45.39	67.22*	
		(17.02)	(19.65)	
Female	212	40.55	66.26*	
		(14.43)	(18.21)	
Male	50	45.44	66.48**	59.92***
		(17.29)	(22.35)	(21.60)
Female	50	40.72	68.88**	54.88***
		(17.87)	(16.41)	(18.43)

* significantly different from pretest, $p < .01$ (partial Eta Squared = .57).
** significantly different from pretest and retention, $p < .01$ (partial Eta Squared = .48).
*** significantly different from pretest and posttest, $p < .01$ (partial Eta Squared = .48).

13.73, $p < .01$. The intrinsic goal orientation scores at the posttest were significantly higher than those at the pretest time for both male and female students.

Attitude. The 2 × 2 mixed ANOVA indicated that there was no significant two-way interaction between gender and time of testing (pretest, posttest) for attitudes toward science learning: $F(1,419) = .36$, $p = .55$ ($n = 421$). There was, however, a significant main effect for time of testing: $F(1,419) = 48.23$, $p < .01$ (see Table 2). The attitude scores at the posttest were significantly higher than those at the pretest time for both male and female students.

Motivation, Attitude, and Science Knowledge

The results of correlation analysis ($n = 374$) showed a moderate positive relationship between the intrinsic goal orientation and attitudes ($r = .42$, $p < .01$) and a small positive relationship between intrinsic goal orientation and science knowledge scores ($r = .21$, $p < .01$). A small positive relationship was also found between attitudes and science knowledge scores ($r = .11$, $p < .05$). There existed a small negative relationship between extrinsic goal orientation and science knowledge scores ($r = -.14$, $p < .01$).

Qualitative Data Findings

Interviews provided insights as to why the students liked or disliked using Alien Rescue. Over 95% of the students interviewed said they en-

TABLE 2. Means and Standard Deviations (in Parenthesis) for Motivation and Attitudes Toward Science

Gender	*n*	Motivation (scale of 1 to 7) Intrinsic Pre-	Post-	*n*	Extrinsic Pre-	Post-	Attitude (scale of 1 to 5) *n*	Pre-	Post-
Male	205	4.73 (1.41)	4.98* (1.29)	202	5.56 (1.30)	5.51 (1.22)	204	3.61 (.67)	3.89** (.81)
Female	215	4.85 (1.32)	5.05* (1.15)	220	5.66 (1.13)	5.58 (1.16)	217	3.57 (.63)	3.81** (.77)

* significantly different from pretest, $p < .01$ (partial Eta Squared = .03).
** significantly different from pretest, $p < .01$ (partial Eta Squared = .10).

joyed using Alien Rescue. The reasons for liking it included, in the order of most frequently cited: (a) learning was fun with Alien Rescue, (b) students were able to use specific hypermedia tools provided in the program, (c) they liked using computers, and (d) they liked working in groups. Students commented: "Having an interactive program to learn through was interesting and fun. I enjoy this type of learning," and "If you just read out of a book, you don't remember it. This way you remember it." A few students said they were frustrated because the problem was difficult to solve and the teachers did not give the answers.

It is significant that a number of students cited being able to work independently and work like a scientist as the most important reasons they enjoyed Alien Rescue. One student stated, "I liked how you got to investigate and hypothesize and experiment to come up with a solution, like a real scientist would. I also liked how you had to figure things out for yourself without a lot of help from the teacher." Another said, "It helps you learn a lot of things because you learn to take notes, which is really important. You learn to be more independent because you have to find out where to go on your own because there is not help. And it's also really fun to research and send up probes and stuff." Although being challenged, students also felt a sense of satisfaction after working hard and being able to solve the problem. "My best experience was when I figured out what planet my alien should go to. I was proud of myself for figuring out the problem."

Students' interest and motivation in using Alien Rescue were reflected in quotes such as: "After I got out of science or just at lunch, me and my friends, we'd talk a lot about where we'd think the aliens should go. When I come back to science, I'd tell my partner what I had learned the previous day and where I was going to research, and what I was going to do that day." Teachers also observed: "Kids are talking about science outside of the classroom. They talk about Alien Rescue in the halls and they talk about it after school. All of the sixth-graders are doing this, and so some of them have friends in different class periods that are working with Alien Rescue. They will say, 'What did you find out today or have you found where this alien can go?' I think that the most exciting thing is that they are talking science outside of the classroom."

When asked what they have learned from using Alien Rescue, students mentioned science concepts as well as research and problem-solving skills. They said: "I've learned to use all of the scientific method, and to really put my mind into it, just concentrating and focusing. It's kind of like you're a real scientist and it brings you to know how to do the specific things like the scientific method, and how to research and collect data."

DISCUSSION

The results of the study showed that the students had significantly increased their science knowledge from pretest to posttest and also retained much of what they had learned after two weeks. Students' attitudes toward science and their intrinsic goal orientation were higher after using Alien Rescue. Students' science knowledge scores were positively related to their attitudes and intrinsic goal orientation; that is, the higher their attitudes and motivation, the higher their science knowledge scores. Such findings indicated that Alien Rescue had a positive impact on the sixth-graders.

There was no gender difference in the posttest or retention test scores. Both male and female students increased their science knowledge understanding after using Alien Rescue. There was also no gender effect on attitudes and motivation. Such results are in line with the findings of other research (Whitehead, 1996). It also confirmed the findings of a previous study that examined the same hypermedia application and found no gender differences in students' performance and their attitudes (Liu, 2004). The interview data indicated that girls were enthusiastic about using Alien Rescue. The few negative responses (as indicated previously) were from boys.

Problem-based learning attempts to capitalize on students' active involvement in the learning process. The data from this study showed that many students liked Alien Rescue because they liked solving this complex problem where they were in control of their learning process and had to rely on themselves, rather than their teachers. Allowing students to take charge and keeping them challenged appeared to motivate them (Hidi & Harackiewicz, 2000). At the same time, hypermedia-based cognitive tools facilitated students' problem solving.

Students' reliance on using the built-in cognitive tools in Alien Rescue was evident in the interviews. Students mentioned the specific tools they used during the process of finding the solution. One student said: "I did research on the aliens first [using the alien database tool] and then I would go to the solar system [using the solar database tool] and find a planet that would match them and write it down in my notebook [using the notebook and bookmark]." Another stated: "After you send out the probe [using the probe builder and launcher rooms] and you get the mass spectrometer, it has the periodic abbreviations so you have to go on the periodic table with them [using the periodic table] and also you have to look under concepts on your toolbar [using the concept database] to find things that you don't know about." These tools have different functions and each offers some assistance to the students. They serve as information resources; means to record, organize, collect, and display data; and allow students to perform activities that would be out of their reach otherwise. As an integral part of Alien Rescue, these hypermedia-enriched cognitive tools provide necessary support to the sixth-graders. Students can access the tools whenever needed. Teachers can spend their time interacting with the students individually, answering questions, and leading class discussions as shown in this study. The findings of the study showed that this hypermedia PBL environment offers sixth-graders a new and effective way of learning–a way that would be difficult to accomplish without the assistance of technology.

REFERENCES

Ames, C. A. (1990). Motivation: What teachers need to know. *Teacher College Record, 91*(3), 409-421.

Germann, P. J. (1988). Development of the attitude toward science in school assessment and its use to investigate the relationship between science achievement and attitude toward science in school. *Journal of Research in Science Teaching, 25*(8), 689-703.

Hendley, D., Stables, S., & Stables, A. (1996). Pupils subject preferences at Key Stage 3 in south Wales. *Educational Studies, 22*, 177-187.

Hidi, S., & Harackiewicz, J. M. (2000). Motivating the academically unmotivated: A critical issue for the 21st century. *Review of Educational Research, 70*(2), 151-179.

Hmelo, C. E., & Ferrari, M. (1997). The problem-based learning tutorial: Cultivating higher order thinking skills. *Journal for the Education of the Gifted, 20*(4), 401-422.

Hoffman, B., & Richie, D. (1997). Using multimedia to overcome the problems with problem based learning. *Instructional Science, 25*, 97-115.

Jarvis, T., & Pell, A. (2002). Effect of the Challenger experience on elementary children's attitudes to science. *Journal of Research in Science Teaching, 39*(10), 979-1000.

Jonassen D. H., & Reeves, T. C. (1996). Learning with technology: Using computers as cognitive tools. In D. H. Jonassen (Ed.), *Handbook of research for educational communications and technology* (pp. 693-719). New York: Macmillan.

Lajoie, S. P. (1993). Computer environments as cognitive tools for enhancing learning. In S. P. Lajoie & S. J. Derry (Eds.), *Computers as cognitive tools* (pp. 261-288). Hillsdale, NJ: Erlbaum.

Liu, M. (2004). Examining the performance and attitudes of sixth graders during their use of a problem-based hypermedia learning environment. *Computers in Human Behavior, 20*(3), 357-379.

Liu, M., Williams, D., & Pedersen, S. (2002). Alien Rescue: A problem-based hypermedia learning environment for middle school science. *Journal of Educational Technology Systems, 30*(3), 255-270.

Mattern, N., & Schau, C. (2002). Gender differences in science attitude-achievement relationships over time among white middle-school students. *Journal of Research in Science Teaching, 39*(4), 324-340.

Miles, M. B., & Huberman, A. M. (1994). *Qualitative data analysis* (2nd ed.). Thousand Oaks, CA: Sage.

Norman, G. R., & Schmidt, H. G. (1992). The psychological basis of problem-based learning: A review of the evidence. *Academic Medicine, 67*, 557-565.

Osborne, J., Simon, S., & Collins, S. (2003). Attitudes towards science: A review of the literature and its implication. *International Journal of Science Education, 25*(9), 1049-1079.

Pintrich, P. R., Smith, D. A. F., Garcia, T., & McKeachie, W. J. (1991). *A manual for the use of motivated strategies for learning questionnaire (MSLQ).* Ann Arbor, MI: National Center for Research to Improve Postsecondary Teaching and Learning, University of Michigan.

Stipek. D. (1993). *Motivation to learn: From theory to practice.* Needham Heights, MA: Allyn & Bacon

Whitehead, J. M. (1996). Sex stereotypes, gender identity and subject choice at A level. *Educational Research, 38*, 147-160.

Wilma D. Kuhlman
Kathy Everts Danielson
Elizabeth J. Campbell
Neal W. Topp

Implementing Handheld Computers as Tools for First-Grade Writers

SUMMARY. All humans use objects in their environment as tools for actions. Some tools are more useful than others for certain people and populations. This paper describes how different first-graders used handheld computers as tools when writing. While all 17 children in the observed classroom were competent users of their handheld computers, their use of handhelds for pre-writing differed among the students. Some students' thinking was clearly enhanced with the use of handhelds before writing. Other students showed writing competence without referring back to their pre-writing work on the handheld. No

WILMA D. KUHLMAN is Associate Professor, Teacher Education Department, University of Nebraska at Omaha, Omaha, NE 68182 (E-mail: wkuhlman@mail.unomaha.edu).
KATHY EVERTS DANIELSON is Professor, Teacher Education Department, University of Nebraska at Omaha, Omaha, NE 68182 (E-mail: kdanielson@mail.unomaha.edu).
ELIZABETH J. CAMPBELL is Elementary Teacher, Rockbrook Elementary School, Omaha, NE 68144 (E-mail: bcampbell@westside66.org).
NEAL W. TOPP is Professor, Teacher Education Department, University of Nebraska at Omaha, Omaha, NE 68182 (E-mail: ntopp@mail.unomaha.edu).

[Haworth co-indexing entry note]: "Implementing Handheld Computers as Tools for First-Grade Writers." Kuhlman, Wilma D. et al. Co-published simultaneously in *Computers in the Schools* (The Haworth Press, Inc.) Vol. 22, No. 3/4, 2005, pp. 173-185; and: *Classroom Integration of Type II Uses of Technology in Education* (ed: Cleborne D. Maddux, and D. LaMont Johnson) The Haworth Press, Inc., 2005, pp. 173-185. Single or multiple copies of this article are available for a fee from The Haworth Document Delivery Service [1-800-HAWORTH, 9:00 a.m. - 5:00 p.m. (EST). E-mail address: docdelivery@haworthpress.com].

Available online at http://www.haworthpress.com/web/CITS

doi:10.1300/J025v22n03_14

students were unable to operate their handhelds in the pre-writing process.

KEYWORDS. Handheld computers, primary children, elementary, writing, handheld educational software, pre-writing process

First-graders in the classroom of a suburban elementary school were comfortably beaming a part of their assignment to each other in March. Because they'd been using their handheld computers since September, these first-graders were competent with many of the options available for them. The researchers' particular purpose for observing in the classroom for the following month was to learn how students used their handheld computers (e.g., PALM, Sony, and CLIÉ) as learning tools, particularly when using them for pre-writing.

Young children come to school with a broad understanding of technology because they don't ever know it is not supposed to be natural, and they see those communication tools in use by the adults around them. Edwards and Willis (2000) define *literacy* as the ability to read and write messages to accomplish the goals of recording and preserving experiences; reflecting upon, exploring, and extending one's thoughts and feelings; and communicating and sharing ideas with others. Incorporating handheld computers as one of the symbolic media of literacy extends it into one more arena beyond traditional visual images of letter drawings, sculptures, letter symbols, paintings, etc. The handheld computer becomes one more tool in the environment useful for literate activities.

HANDHELD COMPUTERS IN SCHOOLS

Norris and Soloway (2003) describe results of using handheld computers with third- through ninth-graders, but some might question whether first-graders could also competently use that technology. Handheld computers are being touted as the future of technology in schools because of reasonable cost for one-on-one access as well as convenience. More educational software continues to be developed for handheld computers.

Effective curriculum is necessary for any technology to be worthwhile in schools (Norris & Soloway, 2003; Pownell & Bailey, 2001). While handheld computer software has some powerful data-processing capabilities that support business uses, educational programs are not as numerous. But this first-grade teacher used some of those built-in capabilities in different ways with her first-graders. For instance, the address book became the alphabetized spelling word list. Students entered their own useful words as well as words that were pertinent to classroom curricula for handy reference when writing. The address book feature was also used to group words into various categories for easy reference. For example, *soccer* was placed in an address book category labeled *sports*. The notepad became a piece of paper on which students drew pictures and wrote words to answer morning work questions. This program replaced the half sheet of scrap paper normally used. The students turned their work in by beaming their notepad document to the teacher's handheld. The notepad was also used for taking notes while on field trips. Students wrote words or drew pictures of what they had observed. Students occasionally used the memo pad for editing practice. The teacher beamed sentences that needed editing to the students. They edited directly on the memo pad and then beamed it back to the teacher's handheld. Thus, the regular curriculum of first-graders became the handheld curriculum; curriculum was not dictated by the technology tool's specialized software.

THE BEGINNING WITH HANDHELD COMPUTERS

The observations took place in a first-grade classroom in a middle-class suburban school district in a large metropolitan area. In the spring of 2001, the teacher borrowed a classroom set of handheld computers from the local university for one week. The class used the handhelds for observing their plant growth in science class. The students drew pictures of their plants each day in a program called Sketchy–educational software developed at the University of Michigan. At the end of the observation period, the students could then run the program like a movie to see their plant growing. The handhelds were also used in a writers' workshop. The students used PiCoMap, a graphic organizer software also developed at the University of Michigan, to plan their story. They then used the planner to write their story on paper. This program was also used for planning their daily journal entries. During language arts, this program was used as a sorting and classifying tool. A PiCoMap was beamed to the students with words from the story of the week. The students then had to manipulate the bubbles in the organizer to sort the words into categories that made sense. Students worked together, and some who struggled with writing on paper with pencils were more successful on the small handheld screen. Another success was the effect on the interactions between students. The first-graders became adept at assisting each other when someone had a problem with a handheld.

As a result of this initial success, the teacher wrote and received a grant for a classroom set of PALM® handheld computers. Putting into place a classroom set of handhelds was a daunting undertaking. A new set of electrical outlets had to be installed in the classroom. A rolling cart was obtained for storage, and three outlet strips and nine triple-plug adapters were used for power to the twenty-five handheld cradles. The handhelds also had to be checked and labeled. Each first-grader was responsible for labeling and checking his/her own handheld computer, and each handheld had to be named and set up with the teacher's laptop for syncing. This process took about two weeks to complete. Once this process was completed, students learned about the day-to-day operations of handhelds. They learned how to remove them from their cradles, hold them, carry and open them, and then replace them properly in the cradles. They also learned the main features of the devices in those small-group sessions. Once everyone had completed this process, the teacher introduced the students to the useful handheld programs in whole group sessions. A camera and projector were used to display the teacher's work on a large screen so the class could view it during instruction.

As the students in this first-grade classroom worked with their handheld computers throughout the year, they became oriented toward ways the computers could be used for different experiences. They were learning the strengths and limitations of the computers–as was the teacher. The capability of beaming was used for almost every lesson. The teacher beamed prepared documents or quizzes to a few students. Those students then spread out and beamed to others. As each student received the document, he/she then beamed the document to another student. Thus, all students had the document or quiz on their handheld computers within one to two minutes.

Technology and Elementary Writers

Lee (2000) surveyed teachers from across the nation about their use of technology in language arts classes and found that many did not believe technology was worth the trouble. Computers that crashed, lack of lab time, and server problems were some of the barriers teachers noted. This first-grade teacher has found that handheld computers mitigate some of those issues (e.g., the need for a lab and server), but crashed computers and lost data can still create problems. First-graders, however, are very flexible and quite willing to move on with another tactic. "Technology has *everything* to do with literacy. And being able to use the latest technologies has *everything* to do with being literate" (Bolter as cited in Wilhelm, 2000, p. 4). As our young students enter the world of reading and writing, they have had multiple exposures to various media and bring to school sophistication about technology that many adults are just now grasping. But, becoming literate is more than watching a television program about reading and writing; it means engaging in literate activities. When technology is a tool toward that end, it can enhance the whole learning process of our already techno-literate children.

HANDHELD COMPUTERS AND WRITING

Students in this first-grade classroom used the capabilities of their handheld computers in different ways in their writing activities, and as Edwards and Willis (2000) predicted, different students found different possibilities for action with those computers as they prepared to write with their computers using the pre-writing tools on their handhelds. Children emerging into literacy naturally manage the symbol systems with differing degrees of competence. Only after they have had many experiences with writing about ideas and events and making lists and drawings to communicate are they ready to consider using a pre-writing organizer. Children in this first-grade classroom wrote every day–usually without handhelds. They wrote in journals, wrote during science about what had just happened in an experiment, and they wrote in math to explain their learning. By April most students were comfortable with the assignments that included writing. Before the researchers' formal observation time, students used the address book often to find words they wanted to spell, and they had occasionally used PiCoMap to organize ideas for writing. The teacher had also decided to have children use the typing option when entering text into their handhelds. She was concerned that learning graffiti might interfere with the students' own developing handwriting skills.

Consequently, observational notes came from children interacting with their handheld computers prior to and during their composing pieces with traditional paper and pencil. Keeping in mind some differences in available writing time during each observation session and different levels of engagement with writing topics, researchers considered the actions and written work of students when using handhelds with two different pre-writing conditions after observing them write without handhelds. These observations began to paint a picture of the competence shown by 17 first-graders. In this article we have retained the original spelling from students' written works to share the developmental nature of their work.

PRE-WRITING STRATEGIES WITH HANDHELDS

These first-graders used both PiCoMap and Sketchy programs as pre-writing tools. As we observed their use of handheld computers under these circumstances, we saw interactions that we interpreted as indicating their differing uses of those computers for action in their classroom. All students used their handheld computers, but they did not use them in exactly the same ways, nor did they achieve the same results in their writing. Some seemed to find the use of handheld computers more helpful than others–perhaps because the handhelds were motivational, perhaps because they were more manageable, or perhaps because they were tools that granted them guidance for the writing task.

When students used PiCoMap as their pre-writing guide, the teacher first modeled the process by talking about how she would write about her grandmother (the main idea in the center oval) and by using details to describe her (the outer ovals surrounding the center oval). The teacher told students to start with a chosen main idea or person in the inner oval and then write details in the outer ovals about that main idea or person.

As students began this pre-writing, they immediately found the appropriate program for the task at hand. No one hesitated or struggled with forming a central oval and then various outgoing bubbles or ovals. In fact, one student drew a strange angular shape and said with a grin on his face, "Even this will make a bubble."

Similarly, before students used Sketchy as a pre-writing tool, the teacher asked them to think about somewhere they had gone and the things they did on that "adventure." After students had shared some of their own ideas, the teacher instructed them to first draw actions on five or six Sketchy frames and then use those actions to help them write their stories. Once again, students chose the correct software and began to draw or write on the Sketchy frames.

STUDENTS' WRITING SUCCESSES WITH HANDHELD COMPUTER PRE-WRITING

Researchers' observations while students were writing and the pieces written indicate that students varied in the ways they used their handheld computers and these particular software pieces as support for writing. One language-delayed student showed delight when she was able to use her Palm®. In previous observations of her writing, this student had avoided the task of writing by sharpening her pencil, washing her hands, and getting a band-aid. The day that she used PiCoMap, she eagerly drew the ovals and wrote a sentence in the circles, one word in each circle: "*Aftrsu, grandma, bakt, cookies*." Although she didn't do precisely what the teacher had told students to do (write the main idea and details about that idea), she eagerly wrote her words, getting some help spelling the words "grandma" and "cookies." Then the teacher drew four boxes on her paper, and the student wrote one word in each box: "*My gra bacing cookes*" This was more writing than she had done in the previous two visits during writing time when students did not use handheld computers.

When this student was ready to start with Sketchy, the teacher initially provided guidance to help her get started sharing about her trip to Disney World. The teacher asked, "What was your first thing?" The student said: "Pack a suitcase. I went last year in Kindergarten. We stayed in a Bed and Breakfast." She used block pieces to draw the suitcase in Sketchy and said, "It was hot. It got to be 100 degrees." She then went on to draw the following pictures and described them as well: Frame 1–She drew a really big black suitcase. "I have two little ones too with toys in it." Frame 2–She played with the circle arc a bit and then drew the bed and breakfast place. "There was no diving board. Mostly in the evening it was hot. There were croaking lizards." Frame 3–She drew the lizard. "This is where it goes in and croaks. I tried to catch them, but I couldn't." Frame 4–She drew a pool. "This is the pool, and there was a drain in that pool."

Although this student never wrote any of this down on paper, she described her trip orally as she drew the pictures. This oral language fluency accompanied her use of the handheld computer. This student's interactions with her handheld and its stylus indicate that she saw the handheld computer as a tool for her literacy. Perhaps drawing was also comfortable for this girl, but she did not limit that to pencil and paper. Her computer was also a tool in the environment that she could use competently for her own literacy.

Some of the students used the PiCoMap pre-writing strategy as the teacher had instructed and wrote pieces that were guided by the connected ideas from the map on their handheld. These students were fluent writers under all circumstances, and the use of handheld computers was workable for them, but did not seem a necessity as a pre-writing tool. Another girl and boy are examples of these students.

This girl used the inner oval for her main idea (Mom) and the outer ovals for ideas about her mother. As she was working on her PiCoMap, she said: "I added arrows. We can make our own arrows on this. They help us to keep our thoughts together so they don't go all around." The importance of focusing on the topic at hand helped her transform her PiCoMap ideas into these sentences she wrote after making her PiCoMap: (/ indicates child's line break.) *I like my Mom. / She is nise. / She helps pepole. / She likes too read storys. / She likes to bakes cokes. / I love mom.* When using Sketchy as pre-writing support, she drew about her trip to the park with very detailed pictures. She said: "I'm going to write about the park. When we click okay, we can't change the names." She further described each of the pictures she had drawn: Frame 1–"I'm drawing a ladder and me going down the slide. We can just draw here with Sketchy. I like it because you can draw a lot of pictures on it, but not more than 50. Wow, I drew a heart as an eye! I can't draw very good on Sketchy, but I like how I draw the sun because the lines make it look really hot out." Frame 2–"Me swinging on the swings." Frame 3–"I'm making a sand castle." Frame 4–"Riding on duck–I forgot the sun" (She then added it). Frame 5–"Hopping stone to stone, there are five but I don't have room." Frame 6–"Little rope thing that you can climb up and climb back down." Frame 7–"I'm playing tag with Emma who is one year older than me. She's eight, but she's really nice. You can write on here too." Frame 8–"I was riding a bike." Frame 9–"I was having a picnic with sandwich, chips, and Sprite." Frame 10–"10, Monkey bars." Frame 11–"I was playing pirates. I know I look kind of weird." Frame 12–"I'm playing on the Merry-go-round. I'm going to need two pieces of paper to write about those 12 things." This girl, as other students in the class, was comfortable with moving through the frames on Sketchy to plan her writing as she remembered her adventure in the park.

This girl used the pictures to help her write the following piece on paper: *Over the weekend I went too the park. / When I got to the park I went down the / slide. And then I swag on the / swings. And then I made / a sandcasle. And I swag on / a boucke. And I Jumpt too / stons. And then climde up / a wallee of bores. And then I / played tag. and then I rod / my bike. and then I had / lounch. and then I did the / mockey bores. and then I played / pirrit's. and then I played / on the merice.*

The boy got right to work with his map after instruction with PiCoMap, and put Ryan as his title and in the center oval. Although he visited some with neighbors while making ovals and typing in words, he kept working with ease. He put play, game, cosin, and run in his outer ovals. This preplanning set up for his writing: *Ryan is my cosin. / Ryan like to play. / He like to play grns. / He like to run fast. / Ryan like to play/ gams.* The close connection of bubbles and final text indicate the boy's use of the handheld's PiCoMap to help him organize his writing.

As did the previously mentioned first-grade girl, this boy had 10 frames in Sketchy for his story about going to Chuck E. Cheese. He did choose to write on the first two frames, an option in Sketchy that is like built-in PALM® Notepad software. Those two frames set the stage with title and author. Frame one is "Chuck E Cheese," and two is "by Author." Frame three is a slice of pizza and the remainder include people and other things, each indistinguishable to anyone but this particular student. His resulting writing is connected to his theme and fits with his setup on the handheld. *I went to Chuck E. Cheese. At Chuck E. / Cheese I eat hamburger / pizza. I like to go / play Ninjas tuttls. / I like to go in the/ tonols. At Chuck E / Cheese I saw to pichshers / thair. I ride with Chuck E. / I played basketball / thair.*

There were a few students in this first-grade classroom who, although very competent with their handhelds, did not seem to find those particular strategies necessary or helpful for their writing. When using only paper and pencil as their tools, two fluent writers seemed to organize their writing in their minds, and they were not noticeably aided by PiCoMap or Sketchy. In fact, after one writer filled in several ovals about her father, she never looked back at the PiCoMap while she was writing the following sentences: *My papa is funny. He calls / Me Walliy dolley. H also calls / Me drerk I say I'm not but / He says you are. When I don't / Now how to turn on the T.V. / Cause they have sepeshle way / To turn it on. He likes glof / Bascetball football fishing and / Swimming. I thick he likes / Soccer I'm not sherow. But I do / Now one thing that he doesn't / Like is dancing and singing. He / Liys some times he hits me / On the head with a pilwwow / And his hand. One time at / His house he hited me on the / Head with a pilwwow but he said / He didn't. He has his on desk / It has a computer a slef coberd / And a kind of desk in front of him.*

Another student's writing seemed somewhat hindered when using PiCoMap and Sketchy. While she had written over 100 words when no handheld was used, her PiCoMap and Sketchy writings were minimal in comparison. With PiCoMap, she had "My friend" in the center oval with "my friend, henry, team, soccer, fany, sit together." Between the time she filled in PiCoMap and the time she wrote her piece, she seemed to have either changed her mind or chose to ignore the pre-writing work. Her written piece contained only 25 words: *Tiffany is my friend. Tiffany / plays with me. Tiffany is nise. / Tiffany plays games with me / Tiffany play rte with me. / Tiffany is a gilr.*

When using Sketchy her drawings were very detailed, but the writing was again sparse with 26 words about a trip to the zoo. Another student continued to write fluently after drawing 10 pictures that seemed to organize her thoughts. She drew detailed pictures of her trip to Aruba. When asked about her pictures, she said: "I went on vacation to Aruba. There's a place that has fishes and then you walk over a bridge to look at them." However, once she finished drawing her pictures, she never looked at them while writing her detailed piece: *In summer I went to Aruaba. / We saw cats lose and parrets. I / Went to the pool. My cosen Madilen / And Andy where there. Madilen / And me saw a brid in the pool. / So we got it out with a stick. / I went on the bech to. There / Was hardly any seaweed. There's / A place where you go and only / Kids go. You can play really fun / Stuff. Like Bingo and uh oh / In Trouble. I got something from / My Mom and Dad. I got some / Bead's. There whor fish to feed / Bread to. And Iqonas running / Aroud And lizzerds. It was / Really really really fun. We stad / There for ten days*

Patterns of Success

Although students responded differently to the writing task with handhelds as a pre-writing tool, all first-graders in this teacher's classroom demonstrated comfort and competence when using their handhelds. When using PiCoMap, most students used the main idea as the center oval and then used other ovals as details about the idea. Different writers used their maps in different ways. When using Sketchy, students moved from frame to frame and either drew or wrote ideas. Again, all of the first-graders operated the software without needing help at that point in the year. Drawing is an important part of emergent literacy, and handhelds afforded students another medium for using that literate action.

For fluent writers, the handheld probably wasn't necessary for pre-writing, although it often helped them to organize their thoughts and brainstorm ideas to write about the topic. For those students who were not as fluent with their writing, the handheld was their literacy tool, and it usually invited them to express literacy in writing or in speaking. Handhelds also seemed to be motivating–students were eager to begin work with them. In fact, one boy chose not to continue writing in the no-handheld setting because he couldn't use the address book to find how to spell words.

GETTING STARTED WITH HANDHELD COMPUTERS

Before bringing this new technology into a classroom, a teacher should be very familiar with the use of the particular handheld computer that will be utilized, as well as be aware of possible uses to help students learn. This teacher completed a graduate course on the subject and read several books and articles before starting the project. Also, she visited with teachers who had such projects underway. Trying to develop a vision for handheld use is important to successful use. Clearly, this first-grade teacher is comfortable and competent with handhelds herself. She is aware of the possible technological glitches and has had to solve problems "on-the-fly." One continuing problem is breakdown of some of the handhelds. Several handhelds stopped working over break, and they had to be replaced with refurbished handhelds, and it took several weeks for their return. This was difficult, because students need to have their own handhelds to gain the full benefit. Time spent using the handhelds during these times was greatly reduced.

In order to facilitate classroom management, an area of the room dedicated to the set of handhelds is important. This area needs to be away from the main traffic of the room, but still convenient for students and teachers to access. The storage area can include cradles for charging the batteries and an area to store the handhelds when not in use. These first-graders were responsible for syncing the handhelds to the teacher's laptop. Two students were assigned each week to complete this process. It does take a fair amount of time for this to be done, and this procedure is still being refined. Security of the devices is an issue that also needs to be addressed.

The use of handhelds in classrooms adds one more element into the learning environment. As with any component of a classroom, handheld use adds to the complexity of the room. Early in the adoption of handhelds, policies and procedures need to be established, such as when the handhelds can be taken home, what can be downloaded onto them, when the device should be synced and backed up, who does this task, and what computer(s) should be used for syncing. Also, policies must be set for any lost or damaged handhelds. These types of management issues need to be addressed and a written policy completed and shared with all involved.

With young children such as these first-graders, additional caution needs to be taken when teaching students how to set their computers into the cradles. The teacher in this study found that when handhelds were not set into the cradle properly (sometimes due to tight fitting cradles or prongs that were slightly askew), some handheld batteries did not recharge and data were lost. It was also vital that students synchronized their work each time they put away their handhelds to avoid those losses. This requires additional time management.

From the beginning of use, students need to understand that this is a learning tool, not a toy. Games should only be played if there is a value tied to the curriculum and the teacher approves. Students need to understand that there are appropriate times to use their handhelds and that the teacher will help them with determining these times. Also, administrators, parents, and the community need to be informed of the intended uses and the value that is expected from these experiences.

CONCLUSION

Handheld computers can be appropriate tools for first-graders. The benefits of using handhelds in this classroom were dramatic for some students. The students who struggled while writing with paper planners had very few struggles when using the handheld. Students were almost always on task with handhelds, and the need for teacher interaction was low. It appears that handheld computers can be used by young writers as supportive tools, particularly for emerging and developing writers. Some students (the least fluent writers) preferred writing on the handheld to actually writing on paper. Others (the somewhat fluent writers) used their handheld to enhance their writing. Still others (the most fluent writers) probably could have written without the pre-writing done on the handhelds, but it was not a deterrent to writing for most of them. Handhelds have also been key in promoting positive interactions between classmates as well as increasing the level of student responsibility.

Even though it is clear to us that children as young as six can benefit from the technology of handheld computers, teachers themselves have to first become users and problem solvers. This is not a new issue in teaching, and inertia is a continual challenge for changes in the educational arena. Teachers have historically taught the way they were taught, and the impetus for change cannot be top-down (Salomon, 1998). This first-grade teacher is now teaching other teachers about using handhelds for instruction. As these small computers become useful tools for teachers, they will be more available as tools for the young students in their classrooms.

REFERENCES

Edwards, C. P., & Willis, L. M. (2000). Integrating visual and verbal literacies in the early childhood classroom. *Early Childhood Education Journal*, *27*(4), 259-265.

Lee, G. (2000). Technology in the language arts classroom: Is it worth the trouble? *Voices from the Middle*, *7*(3), 24-32.

Norris, C. A., & Soloway, E. M. (2003). The viable alternative: Handhelds. *School Administrator*, *60*(4), 26-28.

Pownell, D., & Bailey, G.D. (2001). Getting a handle on handhelds: What to consider before you introduce handheld computers in your schools. *American School Board Journal*, *188*(6), 18-21, 48.

Salomon, G. (1998). Technology's promises and dangers in a psychological and educational context. *Theory Into Practice*, *37*(1), 4-11.

Wilhelm, J. (2000). Literacy by design: Why is all this technology so important? *Voices from the Middle*, *7*(3), 4-14.

Index

For Product Safety Concerns and Information please contact our EU representative GPSR@taylorandfrancis.com Taylor & Francis Verlag GmbH, Kaufingerstraße 24, 80331 München, Germany

* 9 7 8 0 7 8 9 0 3 1 1 0 5 *

T - #0059 - 160425 - C0 - 212/152/11 [13] - CB - 9780789031105 - Gloss Lamination